GET FIT Running

GET FIT

Owen Barder

FIT Running

A & C Black
London

Dedication

This book is dedicated to friends all over the world who I have met through running. You know who you are. Thank you for your friendship and generosity.

Published in 2005 by A & C Black Publishers Ltd
37 Soho Square, London W1D 3QZ
First published in 2002 as *Fitness Trainers: Running for Fitness*

Copyright © 2005, 2002 by Owen Barder

ISBN 0 7136 7204 8

A CIP catalogue record for this book is available from the British Library.

Note: Whilst every effort has been made to ensure that the content of this book is as technically accurate and as sound as possible, neither the authors nor the publishers can accept responsibility for any injury or loss sustained as a result of the use of this material.

Acknowledgements

Cover photograph © Corbis
Photograph on page viii © PhotoDisc. Photographs on pages 7, 8, 20, 34, 48, 103 and 104 © Digital Vision. Photograph on page 72 © Comstock. Photograph on page 88 © David Knight.

Cover and inside design by James Watson

A & C Black uses paper produced with elemental chlorine-free pulp, harvested from managed sustainable forests.

Typeset in 10.75 on 12.75 pt Garamond

Printed and bound in Singapore by Tien Wah Press (Pte) Ltd

Contents

Preface

This is a book about running; but it is also a book about runners. Though I have been around runners for a long time now, they continue to amaze me.

Running has a reputation for being a sport for loners. I do know runners who have quiet determination, a strong sense of self-worth and deep reserves of inner strength. But in my experience, runners are not introverts. They are outgoing, sharing and considerate. Runners seem to have the unusual quality of being equally confident in their own company and in the company of others. To me, this suggests that running can help us to reach an elusive inner balance.

Running is a very honest sport. You get out what you put in. If you haven't done the training for a marathon, you can't fake it. But if you do put in the work, you will reap the rewards. There is nothing flash and nothing glamorous about the sport; just honest hard work. Perhaps this helps to explain the straightforward and open character of the runner.

This book is written mainly for beginners. There is advice to beginners to get you started, and then help for you to progress further, to develop your health, fitness and running. Such wisdom as there is in this book is a composite of my own experiences and those of my friends and fellow runners, who have been kind enough to share what they have learned from many years of running. Like so many others, I have also benefited enormously from the great running writers. There is, in Tim Noakes's words, a shared lore of running from which this book draws; I hope that, in a small way, it also contributes to that community of knowledge.

If this book helps one person to become physically active, or one experienced runner to avoid an injury, or if one jogger is inspired to be the best that they can be, then it will have made a positive contribution to the world. And that is all we can ask of ourselves.

Owen Barder
Berkeley, 2005

1 Why run?

There are many reasons why people of all ages, backgrounds and abilities take up running. For some it is to get fit, to improve their health, to lose weight; for others it may be to improve their self-image or simply for the fun of it.

Fitness

Running is an especially efficient way to increase fitness. Very few other

'Jogging, they say, is competing against yourself. Racing is competing against others. Running is discovering that competing is only competing. It is essential and not essential. It is important and unimportant. Running is finally seeing everything in perspective. Running is discovering the wholeness, the unity that everyone seeks. Running is the fusion of body, mind, and soul in that beautiful relaxation that joggers and racers find so difficult to achieve.'

George Sheehan, Running to Win, *1992*

sports – perhaps only swimming, rowing and cross-country skiing – have such clear benefits in terms of all-round fitness.

Fitness can be measured in many different ways. There are people who can lift huge weights, but could not comfortably run a mile. Weightlifters can generate huge bursts of energy for a short period of time, using their upper body. Some marathon runners, by contrast, would have great difficulty performing simple gymnastics on parallel bars because they lack upper body strength; but they can get themselves around a 26.2-mile course with great efficiency. Both the weightlifter and the marathon runner are fit, in that they can expend energy efficiently, but they are fit in different ways.

One measure of fitness – called *cardiovascular fitness* – is the ability of your body to absorb oxygen and transfer it through the blood supply to the muscles. This is determined by the efficiency of your heart and lungs, and the health of your arteries; it is especially important for endurance sports like running, in which you need to be able to deliver fuel and oxygen to the muscles that do the work.

Fitness tests are generally aimed at measuring your cardiovascular fitness. The results of a fitness test will depend not only on your underlying cardiovascular fitness, but on the specific muscles you use in the test. A trained runner will generally perform better in a fitness test on a treadmill than in a fitness test on an exercise bike.

How will running make me fit?

All fitness is acquired through a process of physical stress and recovery.

When you exercise, your body has to do things that it does not normally do when you are resting. For example, when you run, your heart beats faster, your muscles work harder and your metabolic system burns more fuel. When you stop the exercise, your body recovers and adapts to make it easier to do this in future. It is important to remember that your body's adaptation occurs when you are recovering, not while you are actually undertaking the effort. This is why rest is one of the most important components of any training programme.

Health

As well as increasing your fitness, running improves your health.

Doctors say that you should exercise for thirty minutes a day for three to four days a week. This exercise should raise your heart rate to above 100 beats a minute, or to about 50–75 per cent of your maximum heart rate. Running regularly will increase your life expectancy and improve your quality of life.

Running has been shown to have the following health benefits:

- lower levels of body fat and obesity
- lower risk of heart disease and stroke
- stronger bones, reducing the risk of osteoporosis, osteoarthritis, etc.
- reduced risk of diseases such as cancer and diabetes
- improved immune system
- stronger muscles, and less risk of degradation of joints
- reduced risk of back pain
- reduced incidence of depression and anxiety
- increased co-ordination and mobility, especially in older adults.

Physical exercise is now recognised by the UK National Health Service as a major contributor to good health and an important focus for health promotion.[1] Doctors see exercise as one of the most effective ways to improve the nation's health.

> *Health* means freedom from illness or injury, enabling a person to live normally and in comfort. *Fitness* means the ability to expend a lot of energy efficiently.

Weight loss

Running is an excellent way to achieve lower levels of body fat and improved physical appearance.

According to the National Audit Office, one in five adults is obese, and two-thirds of men and half of women are overweight, causing about 30,000 premature deaths a year in the UK alone. Treating obesity costs the NHS at least nearly £1 billion a year. The wider costs to the economy in lower productivity and lost output are estimated to be a further £2 billion each year. Nearly three in five adults, about 20 million people, need a change in lifestyles.[2] According to the World Health Organisation, 'the spectrum of problems seen in both developing and developed countries is having so negative an impact that obesity should be regarded as today's principal neglected public health problem'.[3]

Running to lose weight

Running is an excellent way to lose weight, reduce body fat and improve your physical appearance. If you eat more calories than you use, your body will store the extra energy as fat. So, put simply, to lose weight, you have to burn more calories than you eat. Running is one very good way to increase the calories you use.

Many runners find that, as their lifestyle becomes healthier, their choice of foods changes naturally and they instinctively begin to prefer more nutritious foods. So while they may still enjoy the occasional blow-out on a tub of ice cream or a plate of fast food, they know that they can do this now and again without feeling too guilty or hating themselves.

Exercise provides a much more positive framework for weight loss than dieting. While dieters often feel perpet-

> 'It is a simple choice. Either I diet, and feel hungry all the time. Or I run regularly, eat exactly what I want, and still control my weight. I feel good about myself.'
>
> *Laura, runner for 6 years*

ually unsatisfied, and suffer from a negative self-image, runners usually benefit from a continuing sense of achievement, self-confidence, and a weight level that can be sustained in the long term without continuing self-denial.

The mental benefits of running

In addition to the health and weight benefits of running, there is good evidence for the psychological benefits of exercise in general, and running in particular. Surveys have shown a strong correlation between being fit and being happy. Exercise reduces anxiety levels and has been found to reduce depression (gentle running is now sometimes prescribed to patients with mild depressive symptoms).

> '**Running is "my time". It's the only time I don't have to give to my boss, my husband, or my daughters. It keeps me sane.**'
>
> *Charlotte, mother of two, marketing manager and superwoman*

Studies of the correlation between exercise and personality produce some striking results. Healthy adults who exercise regularly have greater energy, patience, humour, ambition, emotional stability, imagination, self-sufficiency and optimism, and are more amiable, graceful, good-tempered, elated and easy-going than similar people who don't exercise.

As well as reducing stress through its physical effects, running also creates a space in which we can get time away from sources of anxiety and pressure. Runners are often better able to cope with the pressures of everyday life, partly by permitting a different perspective on minor problems.

> '**Running is the physical break between my work world and my evening that allows me to have personal time with my family and friends.**'
>
> *Phil McCubbins*

Conclusion

I work hard in my job (which is development economics). My colleagues often ask me how I have so much energy. They think that because I have an active lifestyle as well as a demanding career, I should be perpetually tired. The truth is the opposite. My running gives me both physical and mental energy, and the confidence to juggle a busy life.

2 Getting started

Every runner was once a beginner. Nobody I know was born wearing running shoes – we all started out at some point. It is never 'too late' to start running: in fact, many regular runners take it up in their forties or later.

'The miracle isn't that I finished... the miracle is that I had the courage to start.'

John Bingham

Running is simple, cheap and easy, while at the same time being one of the best ways yet invented to get fit, lose weight, improve your self-confidence and meet new friends.

One of the great advantages of running as a sport is that you don't need much to get started. There is no significant equipment to buy (see Chapter 3 for what you'll need). Nor is there a difficult technique to master. You are not dependant on co-ordinating with other people, and you can run at

'Running is a great way to get to know a city! Not only do you get to meet some of the locals but by running through the streets, you learn your way around and even find some cool places you never knew existed! Both of these aspects help to make you feel part of the city!'.

Kathleen Broekhof, 31, from Toronto

any time of day that suits you. The only thing you need to start running is to decide that it is what you want to do.

Do I need medical advice?

In an ideal world, everyone who takes up running should check with a doctor that they are not going to put themselves in danger, but for most runners this is unnecessary.

In my view, you should certainly see a doctor before you start running if you are significantly overweight, over fifty, or if you might be pregnant. Use your common sense, and if you are in doubt, go to your doctor. See the box on page 11.

How much to do at first

So, you've decided to start running, and you've taken medical advice if you need it. You've jumped ahead to Chapter 3 and bought yourself any necessary kit. Now what?

If you are completely new to running, you should not try to do too much too soon. A common error is to think that you should run flat out every time. As we'll see in the training plan in Chapter 5, you should begin by walking, in order to get used to being on your feet. You should build up to running over several weeks, and then only for a few minutes at a time.

The talk test

When you start out as a runner, you should stick rigorously to the talk test: if you cannot talk in complete sentences during your training runs, then you are running too fast.

Many people who are new to running end up with minor injuries in the first six months. These injuries are caused by trying to do too much, or having the wrong shoes. Injury often comes just at the time when new runners are beginning to love their new sport, and it

Should I see a doctor?

See your doctor if any of these apply to you:

- your doctor said you have a heart condition and recommended only medically supervised physical activity;
- during or right after you exercise, you frequently have pains or pressure in the left or mid-chest area, left neck, shoulder or arm;
- you have developed chest pain within the last month;
- you tend to lose consciousness or fall over due to dizziness;
- you feel extremely breathless after mild exertion;
- your doctor recommended you take medicine for your blood pressure or a heart condition;
- your doctor said you have bone or joint problems that could be made worse by the proposed physical activity;
- you have a medical condition or other physical reason not mentioned here which might need special attention in an exercise programme (for example, insulin-dependent diabetes);
- you are middle-aged or older, have not been physically active, and plan a relatively vigorous exercise programme.

If none of these apply to you, you can start on a gradual, sensible programme of increased activity tailored to your needs. If you feel any of the physical symptoms listed above when you start your exercise programme, contact your doctor right away. If one or more of the above is true for you, an exercise-stress test may be used to help plan an exercise programme.

American Heart Association Exercise (Physical Activity) AHA Scientific Position, 1999

can be very frustrating to have to ease off or stop completely.

To avoid injury, you should resist running too much at first, even if you feel ready to go further and faster. In particular, it is a good idea to start off with a month of brisk walking, rather than running. This helps your body to adapt to the effect of regular impact of your feet on the ground, before you start to increase your running mileage.

How to avoid injury when you begin

- if you are new to running, walk for the first month;
- build up slowly; never increase your weekly mileage by more than two miles or 10 per cent, whichever is greater;
- get proper running shoes from a specialist running shop;
- run on grass or trails rather than roads and pavements if possible;
- get advice from experienced runners;
- ignore the feeling in your first three months that you could be doing more;
- see a physiotherapist to get advice on how you might improve your running style.

In Chapter 5 we'll have a look at a training programme to get you started safely from scratch.

Where to run

If you are new to running, one of the first challenges is to figure out where you can run.

Look at a map of your local area, and see what there is in the way of green spaces, such as parks. There are often footpaths alongside rivers and canals. If you know a nearby cycling shop, you may be able to buy a map that shows cycling routes, which are often suitable for running.

There may be running routes for your area on the internet (for example, the Serpentine website – www.serpentine.org.uk – has suggested routes in the London area). There may also be a book with routes for running or walking near you.

Best of all, members of your local running club will know running routes in your area. See pages 15–19 for more information on running clubs.

How to measure the distances of your routes

There are several ways to measure the distances of your running routes:

- if the route is on roads, you may be able to drive a car round them and use the car's distance meter;
- if you have a bike with a cycling computer, you can use this to measure the distance;
- use a map, and either a roller-wheel (which you can buy in a good map shop), which you roll along the route on the map to measure the distance, or a piece of string;
- use an electronic map from the internet, and software such as AccuRoute which measures the distance between points on a map on a computer;
- use a modern pedometer, which measures your distance accurately. These are described in Chapter 3.

Running to and from work

One way to introduce running into a busy life is to run to or from work, or even both. Whether this works for you depends on the distance, and whether you have facilities at work for showering and changing. Some runners keep a selection of clean clothes in the office, which they take in once a week on their rest day, taking home the week's dirty clothes. Many runners find this is the best way to fit running into their day. Often it does not take any more time than travelling on public transport or driving. If you have a long journey, you may find that you can run to or from a railway station or bus stop that is one stop further away from your home.

Goals and motivation

You may want to lose some weight or increase your fitness, to reduce stress and increase your self-confidence, or you may want to achieve a particular time in a race. Effective goal-setting is an important part of increasing your motivation and commitment to running, and getting the most out of the sport.

Your goal should be achievable but challenging. It should be specific, positive, and tied to a particular timeframe. A good goal might be 'lose 5 kg in six months'. A goal such as 'lose some weight' is not sufficiently specific and will not motivate you in the same way. Your goals might be a mixture of longer-term objectives, over a period of months, and shorter-term goals over the coming weeks.

If you decide to aim for a particular race, seek advice from more experienced runners about what you might realistically achieve. The Running For Fitness website (www.runningforfitness.org) will help you to calculate your target times.

Visualise what it will be like to achieve your goal. Promise yourself a reward when you achieve it. Write your goals down, and tell your friends and family about them. This will help to maintain your commitment. You may want to stick a reminder on the fridge.

One of the best ways to motivate yourself is to team up with a friend and agree to do something together. You might both agree to run the same race, for example. Supporting each other will help to reinforce your goal.

> **'Enter a race for motivation. When you start it can sometimes be difficult to keep motivated, especially when it's cold or wet, but if you have a definite target in the form of a race it can be a lot easier. I was a jogger for years, never really improving because I would only go running intermittently, until I entered my first race. Now I race regularly and think of myself as a runner, not a jogger.'**
>
> *Paul Curd, 50, sub-4-hour marathon runner*

Don't become obsessive, or put your goal above your family, friends or health.

Review your goals regularly and adjust them if necessary. If you are injured when you are training, then adjust your goal. Having the wisdom to know when you should adjust your goal is just as important as having the courage and tenacity to overcome challenges on the way.

Training logs

A training log is a diary where you write down every run that you do. OK, it sounds very geeky, but it really is one of the best ways to keep motivated as a runner. A log will help you to track your progress, and to stick to your training programme. Over time, it will be a useful source of information to trace the origins of a period of good running, or of injury and boredom.

Lots of people keep their log in a notebook, or in their diary. This is often the simplest solution. For more technically minded runners, you can also use an electronic diary, such as a palm-top; or use a spreadsheet on your PC. There is software you can get for your computer, and there are websites you can use to record your training online. See overleaf for an example of a training log.

Joining a running club

I love running on my own, because it gives me some precious time to myself. But I also love being a member of a running club.

Running clubs are *not* full of super-fit, super-fast athletes. You do not have to be fast to join: whatever your standard, you will be welcome, and you will find that there are plenty of members who run more slowly than you do.

There are a number of benefits from joining a running club. You will:

- meet other runners, and so be encouraged to run regularly;
- get advice from experienced runners on how to start running, how to avoid injury, how to improve, good routes to run in your area;

January 2005: Week 3

	Run	Miles	Time	Type	Overall	Conditions	Notes
Sun 16 Jan	Richmond Park	10	1:41	LSD	7	Overcast	Ran with Simon. Felt strong until 8 miles; need more gels?
Mon 17 Jan	Rest	–	–	Rest	–	–	Legs a little stiff this morning.
Tue 18 Jan	Bridge loop	5	0.43	Tempo	5	Cold morning	2 miles at 8:15/mile. Very hard work.
Wed 19 Jan	Rest	–	–	Rest	–	–	Took it easy after a hard day yesterday.
Thu 20 Jan	Office to home	4	0.42	Recovery	7	Drizzle	Ran easy; felt good. Tough day in the office.
Fri 21 Jan	Track	4.5	0.36	Intervals	8	Overcast, bit windy	3 sets of 3 x 800 m. Target: 4:00 per 800 m. Kept even pace.
Sat 22 Jan	Battersea Park	3	0.28	Recovery	7	Cold	Wet ground. Took it easy after track.
Weekly totals		**26.5**	**4:10**				

Weight 78 kg
Resting heart rate 64 bpm

January 2006: Week 4

	Run	Miles	Time	Type	Overall	Conditions	Notes
Sun 23 Jan	Richmond Park	11	1:55	LSD	8	Clear, crisp	Took 3 gels: felt strong whole way. Lovely day.
Mon 24 Jan	Battersea Park	3	0:30	Recovery	7	Clear again	Slight niggle left ankle.
Tue 25 Jan	Rest	–	–	Rest	–	–	Ankle fine today.
Wed 26 Jan	Office to home	4	0:40	Recovery	8	Warm	Could have run forever. Bumped into Susannah on bridge.
Thu 27 Jan	Bridge loop	5	0:44	Tempo	8	Warmer	Much better than last week. 2 miles at 8:15'/mile – felt easier.
Fri 28 Jan	Rest	–	–	Rest	–	–	Swimming lesson in evening.
Sat 29 Jan	Hills in Greenwich	4	0:37	Strength	5	Humid	Wet ground. Last rep on each hill was a killer. Karen v. inspiring.
Weekly totals		27	4:26				

Weight   73 kg
Resting heart rate   65 bpm

- get motivation and enjoyment from running with other people, and the miles will slip past on your long runs;
- meet new people from all walks of life; and
- get discounts at running shops and on race entries.

Depending on the club, you may also get access to coaching, regular races and competition (if you want it) and an opportunity to be part of a team. Some clubs provide access to physiotherapy, and information such as newsletters and seminars.

Questions to ask when you join a running club

Any club worth joining will welcome visitors – just show up for one of their runs and see if you like it. Here are some questions you might ask yourself:

- Where are they based? How hard is it to get to the meeting point from home or work? Are the runs somewhere pleasant?
- What are the facilities like? Do they have changing facilities or a clubhouse?
- How serious is the club? Some clubs tend to be quite serious, some less competitive. Is it too competitive for you? Not serious enough?
- What sort of running do they do? Do they do road running, marathons, cross-country and track and field? Which are you interested in?
- When are their club runs? Are they at a convenient time? Are they on a convenient day of the week?
- What sort of people are they? Will you enjoy spending time with them? Do they organise social events?
- How much does it cost?

Some new runners make the mistake of thinking that they should wait until they are faster and more experienced before they join a club. Some clubs will have one or two fast megastars, but these will easily be outnumbered by members who run to control stress, keep fit, lose weight or just to socialise. Don't be daunted about joining a club. Every one of its members was a beginner at some time. Any club will be glad to welcome new people into the sport.

'My running club is the only reason I stay here in London. It is the best way to meet people of all different ages, from every walk of life.'

Simon, 32, from New Zealand

You can get information about running clubs in your area from a local specialist running shop, or from UK Athletics (see page 110 for address details).

Conclusion

Your first steps as a runner are the most important. They will determine whether running becomes a lifelong pleasure, or a temporary, injury-laden aberration. Once you lace up a pair of running shoes and get outside, you will find that it is much easier, and more rewarding, than you imagined it could be. The biggest obstacle is likely to be that you try to do too much too soon.

Somewhere near you there is a community of runners, each of whom was once a beginner. If you want to sustain running as part of your lifestyle, learn from the experience of others, and enjoy a broader social life, you should consider linking up with colleagues or friends who run, or joining a local running club. Summon up the courage to go along: it is a decision you will never regret.

Kit

You don't need to invest much in kit and accessories. All you really need is a decent pair of running shoes and (if you are a woman) a suitable sports bra. It would be a huge mistake to think that you can get by without either of these.

Shoes

What shoes to buy

There is no such thing as a better 'make' or 'model' of shoes. A good pair of running shoes is one that suits your particular running style; and a bad pair is one that does not.

Your body generally comes with some complicated machinery as standard – muscles, tendons, ligaments, joints, bones – which enable you to walk and run. Your ability to run efficiently and injury-free depends in part on the alignment and operation of these moving parts. Your individual biomechanics are partly determined by your genes, but also by your lifestyle, past injuries, treatment and exercises. Running shoes vary according to the way and extent to which they accommodate different biomechanics, and your choice of running shoes should depend on your personal biomechanical profile.

Paradoxically, the best runners often don't need to spend much money on running shoes. Because they usually have the good luck to have good biomechanics, their running style does not require them to buy shoes that correct the way in which their feet roll when they hit the ground, or cushion them from the stress on their joints as their feet repeatedly hit the ground. The rest of us mere mortals, however, need shoes that will correct our deficiencies and weaknesses, and improve our running action so that every footstep does not place an intolerable pressure on our feet, legs and pelvis.

Motion control

When your heel hits the ground, the foot naturally rolls in from the outside edge. This rolling is called *pronation*, and is a natural and desirable part of the running action, since it helps to absorb the impact of running. Think of it like the way that parachutists bend their knees and roll as they hit the ground.

Although some pronation is desirable, around three-quarters of runners *overpronate* – that is, their feet roll in too much. Persistent overpronation causes a variety of injuries: stress in the ankle and Achilles tendon, shin splints, knee pain, torn hamstrings, hip strains, or pain in the lower back.

Just before the take-off phase of running, the foot rolls back towards the outside. This is called *supination*. As with pronation, this is a normal part of the running action. But a small minority of the population – less than 10 per cent – *oversupinate*. This can also cause a range of overuse injuries over time.

Excessive pronation and supination may be caused in part by problems in the feet; but they are usually also symptoms of imbalances or weaknesses elsewhere in the body, including in the back, hips, buttocks, hamstrings, quadriceps and knees. While the right running shoes can help to limit the effect of these biomechanical deficiencies, it is better if possible to identify and correct the underlying causes.

Runners who are lucky enough neither to pronate nor supinate excessively are called 'neutral'. They don't need special shoes to correct their running, which often means that they can wear lighter and cheaper shoes than the rest of us.

Running shoes come in the following categories:

- **Motion control:** most aggressive at preventing overpronation.
- **Stability:** help to limit overpronation, but not as much as motion control.
- **Neutral:** for runners who don't need their shoes to prevent bio-mechanical weaknesses.
- **Supinators:** for the minority of the population who oversupinate.

These running shoes all seem basically the same at first, but when you look at them carefully they have different components built into the shoe according to the extent to which they are designed to control the movement of the foot.

Cushioning

Good cushioning is important because it reduces the shock that is transmitted through the foot to the lower leg, knee and hip joints. As well as reducing the risk of injury, cushioning improves the comfort of running. Heavier runners, and those doing big mileages on roads or pavements, should ensure that their running shoes have sufficient cushioning.

However, cushioning makes the shoe heavier and, because it absorbs energy, it can reduce your running efficiency. For most of us the effect on performance is tiny; and the benefit of more comfort and safety when running more than outweighs the loss of performance. But some runners will also use 'racing flats' for important races (see overleaf).

Different manufacturers have different cushioning technologies. Some use pockets of air to absorb impact; others use gels or spongy plastics. You should try these for yourself and see which you find most comfortable.

'When I first started running, I used a pair of old plimsolls. It did my knees no good whatsoever. I recommend that you go to a good running shop and get a decent pair of trainers.'

Malcolm French

Other types of shoe

As well as regular trainers, other running shoes available include:

- **Racing flats:** very little cushioning, and usually not much motion control, but lighter than shoes you might use for regular training. Unless you are very concerned about your performance, or have very good biomechanics, racing flats are generally best left to the professional athletes.

- **Track spikes:** for training on the athletics track. They have short spikes under the toes that grip the track. The shape of the shoe forces you to run on your toes, which is more efficient on short distances (though harder on your legs). Track spikes have very little cushioning or motion control.

- **Cross-country spikes:** longer spikes than track shoes, to give you more traction on soft ground; like track shoes they have little cushioning because they are usually used on softer ground and because the lack of cushioning gives them more stability on uneven ground. They also have little motion control. Because of the spikes, they cannot be used on hard surfaces. The spikes are replaceable, and different length spikes are used depending on the nature of the surface.

- **Fell shoes:** designed for running off-road, for example on mountain trails; they usually have good grips on the bottom of the shoe, such as studs. Like cross-country spikes, they generally have little cushioning and motion control, because they are designed for use on softer, uneven ground.

These specialist running shoes are not generally available in high-street sports shops. For a good selection, and good advice, you should go to a specialist running store, where you will be given individual advice on your needs.

How long do shoes last?

You sometimes see inexperienced runners looking at the bottom of a running shoe to see if it needs replacing, for example by seeing whether it has much 'tread' left. This is a mistake: the main determinant of the longevity of a shoe is not the wear to the outer sole; it is the compression of the mid-sole, which is the spongy layer between the outer sole and your feet. The material that is usually used to make mid-soles is

> 'Buy a new pair of shoes every 300 miles or so: in the end it will save you money because you won't have to pay out a lot of money for physio treatment.'
>
> *Rachel Broster*

light and absorbs shock well, but it gradually compacts as it is used, which reduces its shock absorbency and gradually distorts the shoe. As a result of the compression of the mid-sole most running shoes have an average life expectancy of about 300–600 miles. Very heavy or uneven runners might wear out part of the outer sole before the mid-sole is too compressed, but this is unlikely.

The actual life of your shoes depends on your weight and your running style. You can see whether your shoes are past their best by looking at the compression lines along the side of the shoe, and seeing whether the mid-sole can be compressed with pressure from your thumb. If you can no longer compress the mid-sole, then it is time to replace your shoes. If you begin to get any kind of ache or pain in your ankle or knee, check that your running shoes don't need replacing.

Incidentally, you should not put your running shoes in the washing machine, nor use very hot water to clean them. The hot water damages the shoe, especially the mid-sole, and leads to distortion in the shape of the shoe. For the same reason, you should avoid drying wet shoes on a very hot radiator.

Many runners keep track of the life of their running shoes in their training log, and use this to warn them when they are likely to need a new pair.

Where to buy running shoes

You should buy running shoes from a specialist running shop if possible. At a good running shop, the staff will help you to pick shoes that fit your own running style and help to control your biomechanical weaknesses. They may have specialist equipment for this (e.g. a treadmill with sensors to detect how your feet hit the ground) or they may watch you run up and down the street outside.

Such shops are usually a little more expensive than high-street stores, but they usually offer discounts to members of running clubs on production of a membership card. However, their staff are much more knowledgeable and patient than your average teenager in a Saturday job; and they are usually runners themselves. It is a false economy to save a few pounds on running shoes if the result is that you get a pair that are not right for you, and end up injured.

Clothing

Sports bras

All women should wear sports bras when they run. The ligaments that support your breasts can be permanently stretched and damaged if your breasts are not properly supported during exercise. This leads to droopy breasts, and cannot be reversed. A good sports bra provides support for your breasts to prevent them from bouncing while you run. In addition, surveys show that half of women who exercise suffer from breast pain, and this is often a reason why some of them give up.

The best way to choose a sports bra is to get expert advice. There are specialist retailers in the UK such as www.lessbounce.com who can talk you through the details by phone or by email.

You should not buy your bra based on a measurement of your bust size. Bras from different manufacturers are not all the same size. Your measurement may have been done badly, or your bust size may have changed

> 'The right sports bra for you is one that fits you comfortably and significantly reduces the movement of your bust when running. Every woman's bust is different, so what works for your training partner, may not be right for you.'
>
> *Selaine Messem, owner,*
> *www.lessbounce.com*

(especially if you increase your training, which tends to reduce your cup size). Your optimal fitting can also vary over your menstrual cycle (because of water retention). Instead you should try the bra and choose one that is comfortable for you and that fits you snugly. Check that there are no seams or clips that will irritate your skin over a long run. Jump up and down – your breasts should hardly bounce at all. Make sure that the base of the bra will not ride up over your breasts while you are running, but that it is not so tight that it makes breathing difficult. You should also find out whether the shoulder straps cut in.

After running, particularly on long runs, some women have sore skin between their breasts, across the back under the strap and fastener, or along the line of the base of the bra under the breasts. This friction can be reduced by liberal application of Vaseline, or some other lubricant, on these areas before you start running.

A crop top is not the same as a sports bra, and many of them don't provide the support you need. However, there are some sports bras that are designed to look like crop tops so that you can run in them without a t-shirt over the top.

A number of manufacturers also make sports bras that are designed to accommodate the sensor strap of a heart rate monitor, to prevent you from having to have two separate straps around your chest.

Like running shoes, you should replace your sports bras from time to time – with a lot of use they can last less than a year. Check regularly to see if your bust is moving more than it should, or if you are beginning to get breast pain. You may also find that your bra begins to rub after a while.

T-shirts and shorts

You'll need some shorts and t-shirts for running. At first you can just dig out some old summer clothes, but over time you may want to get some clothes specifically for running.

Steer well clear of cotton for running clothes. When cotton gets wet (from sweat, or from rain) it gets heavy, irritates the skin, does not insulate well and dries slowly. Sports clothes manufacturers have come up with synthetic materials that help to keep you dry by mov-

> '**Running in wet cotton t-shirts always rubs my nipples until they bleed, and I end up looking as if I've been in a road accident.'**
>
> *Geoff Higham, 31*

ing the water from the surface near the skin to the outer layer where it can evaporate (this is known as wicking). These 'technical' materials really do help to keep you dry, warm in cold weather and cool in warm weather; but they are also more expensive than regular material. Some runners find that they retain body odour more than other materials, even when washed.

For t-shirts, you will need some short-sleeved and long-sleeved shirts depending on the weather. If you use t-shirts made of technical materials, then don't wear a cotton t-shirt as well for warmth, since this prevents the sweat from evaporating through the technical clothing. Instead, get a long-sleeved, thermal, technical top for running in the cold.

Your choice of shorts is a matter of personal preference. Some runners prefer to wear tight shorts (like cycling shorts but without the padding) because they reduce friction between the thighs. Others prefer baggier shorts. Lots wear both: the tight shorts underneath to reduce friction, with baggy shorts over the top – a combination that is less revealing but can get hot. If you are running in a foreign country, think about local sensibilities and customs before setting off in only a pair of skin-tight, figure-hugging cycling shorts.

You can also wear running tights, which may come down to your knees, calves or toes. These keep you warm in cold weather, and are sometimes worn by runners who prefer not to display their legs. Again, some runners accompany these with a pair of baggy shorts over the top.

Underwear

You would be surprised how many new runners want advice on what – if anything – to wear under their shorts.

Men's running shorts usually include an inner liner, designed to support their equipment, so men don't in general wear underpants under their running shorts.

Some women's shorts and running tights are lined and have proper gussets – these can be worn without knickers underneath if you want. Otherwise, there is often a seam just where you don't want it, which would be very uncomfortable without underwear. Many women wear knickers under their running shorts or tights in any case, for comfort or in case their shorts are otherwise too revealing (especially since some materials become quite see-through when wet).

When it is very cold, runners (of both sexes) sometimes wear thermal underwear under their shorts to keep warm. The key to good thermal underwear is that it should be windproof. Helly Hansen makes thermal underwear designed for sports, available in both men's and women's versions.

Clothes for cold weather

In cold weather, the best approach is to dress in many light layers. In general you should have a synthetic base layer that wicks sweat away from your skin, with a windproof or water-resistant top layer. On very cold days, you may need an additional thermal layer in between. Using layers enables you to keep warm with the least weight of clothes, and enables you to regulate your temperature quickly and easily by adding or removing layers as you want.

You may also want to use some light gloves. The thin nylon type work well (cotton and woollen gloves are not sufficiently windproof and can become waterlogged). You can get gloves for runners which are fluorescent yellow, or which have reflective material for running in the dark.

For running when it is cold, you may want a hat. A regular woollen hat will do, or a baseball cap made of synthetic material. Again, you can get water-resistant caps, which are useful if it is drizzling; and you can get bright and reflective hats which ensure that you are seen in traffic.

When you choose a raincoat, you will have to trade off three considerations: the extent to which the jacket is waterproof, its breathability (i.e. whether it retains your perspiration) and its weight. On the whole, I find jackets made of fully waterproof materials, such as Gore-Tex™, are too heavy for running. They also tend to be insufficiently breathable, becoming damp inside because the sweat does not evaporate properly. But breathable jackets are rarely fully waterproof: they might protect you from a shower, but will not be much use in heavy rain. So I prefer a raincoat that is windproof and showerproof, but not fully waterproof. This helps to keep me warm in the rain, and I figure I'm going to get wet whatever happens.

> 'There is no such thing as bad weather for running: only the wrong clothing.'
>
> Grethe Petersen, 36, from Denmark
> (and the author's partner)

One excellent option for bad weather is a gilet, which is a waistcoat-shaped jacket made from water-resistant material that protects your torso but not your arms. This can keep you warm in rain and wind, while allowing your sweat to evaporate. A body-warmer is a waistcoat-shaped thermal top for keeping your torso warm.

As well as a suitable jacket, many runners (male and female) use running tights for cold weather, long-sleeved thermal tops, and if necessary thermal underwear (see page 29).

Clothes for hot weather

In hot weather, you should not strip down to the bare minimum, because you must make sure that you protect your skin from the sun. Sunscreen can be annoying, because it blocks your pores and so prevents you from sweating, and also runs into your eyes, but it is a lot better than skin cancer. On long runs, remember to refresh your sunscreen regularly, in case it is being washed away by sweat. If possible, block the sun using a sunhat and t-shirt so that you don't have to rely on suntan lotion. Use zinc cream (as favoured by cricketers) to protect your face from the sun.

Timing and distance measurement

Watches

Most runners use a watch with a stopwatch function to measure how long they run.

Sports watches with a lap function are useful for races, so that you can check your speed at each mile marker. They are also useful if you train on the track where you need to monitor carefully the speed of your efforts, and your recovery times between efforts. Some runners use a repeat 'countdown' function that enables them to programme their watch to bleep at regular intervals, to pace themselves while they are running (e.g. every 25 seconds if they are running 100 second laps) or to regulate their recovery times.

Features in a good running watch

- a large display, so that you can see it while you are running, and a light so that you can see it in the dark;
- a stopwatch with a lap function, preferably one that can store 10 or more laps in its memory;
- water resistance, for running in the rain;
- easy-to-press buttons, so that you can press the lap button during a race or on the track.

Heart rate monitors

Heart rate monitors consist of two components: a chest strap (sensor) and watch (receiver). The straps can be bought separately when you need them for around £30. The watch usually has the normal functions of a sports watch, as well as the heart rate functions.

You can use heart rate monitors to adjust your training; to track your progress as you become fitter; to check for overtraining; and to help you judge your pace. They are, however, expensive, and they are certainly not a necessary piece of equipment unless you choose to base your training on heart rate training zones.

Serious runners may want a heart rate monitor that can download stored data from the watch to a personal computer, using either a special interface unit or a microphone. This allows the runner to store and analyse the data from each session. There is one brand that downloads data straight to a specially equipped mobile phone.

Some heart rate monitors estimate the number of calories used in each workout, based on your gender and weight. This can help to provide additional motivation, although the calculations are not very accurate.

Pedometers and speed and distance monitors

Older and cheaper pedometers work by counting the number of steps taken, and then multiplying by the average stride length. This approach is not very accurate, because your stride length depends on how fast you are going, how tired you are, and the terrain on which you are running.

In the last few years, new types of distance monitors have become available which provide much more accurate estimates of the distance you run (and therefore your speed). These can work in one of two ways. The models from Nike and Polar include a small sensor that you tie into your shoelaces, which measures the acceleration of your feet and calculates your speed. The model from Timex includes a receiver that you wear on your arm or belt that tracks its position using international navigation satellites.

In either case, the sensors transmit information about distance and speed to a watch worn on the wrist. This means that you can see your speed and distance in real time as you are running.

Both methods are quite accurate (within 1 per cent), and can help you to train more effectively by providing information about the distance you have run and your speed. They are, however, quite expensive.

Other kit

You will find a range of useful items in your local specialist running shop, including:

- a wrist wallet, or a small shoe pocket that goes into your shoelaces, to carry your door or car key and some spare money for emergencies;
- a bottle for carrying water on long runs; this can be either a doughnut-shaped bottle that goes round your hand (made by Runners' Aid) or a bottle that fits into a specially designed belt around your waist;
- a reflective vest, and wrist and ankle reflective straps, for running at night (you can get ankle straps with flashing lights on them in some bike shops);
- an identity tag to identify you in case of emergency, including any emergency medical information (e.g. allergies, blood group); you can either get this from a medical identity company such as MedicAlert, or you can do it yourself by getting a dog tag made (your local key-cutter can engrave one for you) with your name, phone number and any essential medical details;
- plasters for blisters – these are different from the normal plasters you get in chemists, as they are specifically designed to promote healing of blisters. Recommended brands of plaster specifically for blisters are Compeed and Second Skin;
- Vaseline (or another lubricant), which is used to prevent chafing in long runs; runners often apply copious quantities of Vaseline to the nipples, between the thighs, and under the arms towards the shoulder blades, all of which are areas that can rub.

4 Special considerations

Women runners

More and more women are taking up running: about half the members of my running club are women. Running empowers and liberates us all, giving us space to change our perspective. However, there are some areas that women need to give particular consideration to.

Shoes

Women have wider hips and shoulders compared to men; they are, on average, shorter and lighter than men, and they have about 8–10 per cent more body fat. As a result of the shape of the pelvis, women's legs are turned outwards more than men's, and women have a greater propensity to suffer from knee and hip injuries.

This means that women and men get different types of running injuries, and the appropriate treatments are slightly different. On average, women suffer more than men from pain in the knee area.

Because of these physical or biomechanical differences, you would think women's running shoes ought to be designed to be rather different from men's. There are running shoes made especially for women, but studies have found that they don't make as much difference as you would expect. They are generally more comfortable, however, because they are designed for narrower feet.

Personal safety

There are a number of steps that women can take to minimise the risks to their personal safety while running.

Staying safe

- carry a mobile phone, so that you can call for help if you need it; you can also carry an inexpensive rape alarm (mace and pepper sprays are not legal in the UK);
- avoid remote and unlit areas, and keep away from trees and bushes;
- vary your routine, so that you don't always run the same route at a predictable time;
- avoid using headphones while running; listening to music makes it more difficult to hear strangers coming up behind you (as well as making you more vulnerable to cars, dogs, roller-bladers, etc);
- make sure someone knows where you are going and when you are expected back; make sure they know what to do if you don't return in good time;
- don't wear expensive jewellery that might attract unwelcome attention.

Nutrition for women runners

We will look at a balanced diet for runners in Chapter 6. However, there are a few issues that affect women more than men.

First, you should ensure that you get enough iron in your diet. Iron is essential for transporting oxygen through your bloodstream, as well as providing a key building block of muscle tissue. It is easy for women to become anaemic (i.e. have insufficient iron) because of their periods. If you don't eat red meat, make sure that you get iron from sources such as dark green vegetables, beans and dried fruit. Avoid drinking coffee or tea with your meals, as these interfere with the absorption of iron. Watch carefully for the symptoms of anaemia, which include fatigue, palpitations, dizziness, dryness of mouth, sores in the corner of the mouth and brittle hair. Your doctor can easily test for iron deficiency. If necessary take a food supplement to maintain your iron levels.

Second, you should ensure that you have enough calcium. This is essential for building strong bones, and avoiding osteoporosis; it may also help to reduce high blood pressure. Dairy products are generally a good source of calcium; if you don't eat dairy products then try to buy calcium-fortified alternatives (you can buy calcium-fortified mineral water, orange juice and soya milk, for example).

Third, some women runners don't eat enough fat. You need some fat in your diet, not least to ensure that you have healthy hair and skin. Remember that some fats are good for you – try to increase your intake of mono-unsaturated fats (e.g. from olive oil and nuts) and essential fatty acids (e.g. from oily fish and seeds) while avoiding saturated fats (which mainly come from animal products). Insufficient fat is highly correlated with irregular periods, which can have long term health repercussions.

Eating disorders

The number of women suffering from *anorexia nervosa* and *bulimia nervosa* is growing in many Western societies. People with anorexia nervosa restrict their food intake and have a distorted image of their bodies. A person with bulimia nervosa may also restrict food intake, but binge occasionally, usually following this with self-induced vomiting or the use of laxatives.

On the negative side, compulsive running can be a symptom of an eating disorder. On the positive side, running can improve your self-image and help to control body weight without resort to unhealthy eating habits.

Compulsive exercising, including running, can be a symptom of bulimia. Running can be a popular sport for women on the margin of bulimia, because it is such an effective way of burning calories.

It is sometimes difficult to recognise the early symptoms of eating disorders, especially in yourself. It is important for people close to us – particularly family and good friends – to pay attention. While it is normal for competitive athletes to pay attention to their weight, some women runners may become fixated on their body weight. If you suspect that you, or someone close to you, may be suffering from an eating disorder, you should seek expert help right away. Anorexia and bulimia are serious illnesses, and can be very damaging and, in extreme cases, fatal.

You may know people who don't suffer from an eating disorder but who are a little bit too obsessive about what they eat. Perhaps you are one yourself. They sometimes live under a tyranny of counting every calorie, or every gram of fat. This can be stressful for them, and those around them, and can be unhealthy if they are too restrictive in what they eat because they don't get a balanced diet containing all the nutrients, vitamins and minerals that they need. It is also frequently self-defeating: all too often they will go hungry throughout the day, eating too little for breakfast and lunch, and are so hungry by the end of the day that they eat too much. It is more healthy to eat a large breakfast, and then to eat little and often throughout the day.

Running and self-image

In general, exercise is a much less damaging, and more sustainable, way to lose weight than dieting. Controlling what you eat can be negative, destructive and unhealthy; while managing your weight through exercise promotes a positive self-image, confidence, and a healthy, sustainable lifestyle.

Running and periods

Many women runners find that exercise can improve their mood and reduce discomfort before and during their periods. Moderate exercise, such as running, can relieve the physical symptoms of pre-menstrual tension, including tender breasts. However, some women

A runner's journey from an eating disorder

'It has been a journey of sorts over the course of nearly nine years. Something like a long, hard cross-country course: undulating, rough ground, changeable weather – sometimes for and sometimes against!

'What started out as a very negative and destructive relationship between food and running turned a corner and developed into a solid working partnership. Running alone helped me to gain self-reliance, strength and self-confidence. Little by little I learned that to build on these traits required nourishment, both physically and emotionally, and that running tended to both these needs. Whereas running used to be a weapon used against food, slowly and gently it became an ally. Fuelling-up appropriately and pushing myself to finish a hard run, knowing and trusting that my body will carry me through to a strong finish instead of ending a race with feelings of emptiness and weakness, is truly an empowering feeling. It's given me the sense that, through effort, sheer hard work and respect for both others and myself, anything is possible!'

Nia Parry, 31, London

runners may experience irregular or missed periods from time to time, a condition that is normal but can lead to long-term health problems if it persists. It can be avoided if you look after yourself and eat well.

On the whole, unless you are sure that your period affects your running, there is no strong reason to adjust your running around your menstrual cycle. However, if you are an endurance athlete, and you suffer from water retention and weight gain at certain times during your cycle, this may reduce your performance at particular times of the month.

For some women runners, particularly those training for long distances, running can lead to *amenorrhea* – erratic or absent periods. This seems to be caused by some combination of low body fat, inadequate nutrition and stress. Exercise-induced amenorrhea is generally temporary, and periods return when the training load is reduced. But women who run intensively should be aware of the long-term negative impact because it increases the chances of osteoporosis. There is also evidence of lower bone density in women who miss their periods; and this can lead to increased risk of stress fractures and brittle bones later in life.

If you start to suffer from irregular periods, you should see a gynaecologist, both to rule out other, more serious, causes, and to try to identify steps that you can take to restore your normal cycle. Look carefully at your diet, to ensure that you are getting enough calcium, protein and fat, and consider whether you are suffering from other symptoms of overtraining, such as elevated heart rate, insomnia or fluctuating weight. Persistent amenorrhea can be treated with hormone therapy.

If you become a more serious runner, it is worth keeping track of your periods in your training log, in case you are one of those runners whose performance is affected by your menstrual cycle.

Running and pregnancy

Most doctors now agree that moderate exercise during pregnancy is good for both mother and baby. Women who exercise before and during pregnancy generally have less complicated pregnancies and births.

> 'I kept running until six weeks before my daughter was born. Just run how you feel, and listen to both your bodies. I started running again a week after Emily was born. Fortunately, she loves endorphins in her milk!
>
> *Swenja Surminski, London*

However, you should not continue to run during pregnancy as if absolutely nothing has changed. Your body changes when you are pregnant. For example, ligaments and bones soften, to accommodate the baby, which means that you are more susceptible to injury. Your temperature regulation mechanisms are strained, which means it is easier to overheat, which could damage the foetus, especially in the early stages of pregnancy. You should avoid intensive exercise with high heart rates to avoid depriving your baby of oxygen.

You should check with your doctor before running while pregnant, both to discuss general guidelines, and to check that you are not particularly at risk.

If you develop any of the following symptoms, you should stop running immediately and consult a doctor:

- bloody discharge or amniotic fluid leakage from the vagina
- sudden swelling of the ankles, hands or face
- persistent, severe headaches or visual disturbance
- swelling, pain and redness of the calf in one leg
- elevation of pulse rate or blood pressure that persists after exercise
- excessive fatigue or any palpitations or chest pains
- persistent contractions (they may suggest the onset of premature labour)
- unexplained abdominal pain
- insufficient weight gain.

If you do decide to continue to run, here are some guidelines:

- don't run to exhaustion; and don't run at high levels of intensity (e.g. sprinting) which may affect the baby's oxygen supply;
- be careful not to overheat, especially during the early weeks;
- be careful not to dehydrate: you may need to drink more water than you are used to;
- maintain your blood sugar levels: you should eat more than you are used to;
- don't try to stick to a training schedule: run as you feel inclined and listen to your body and to your baby;

- you might want to use a heart rate monitor to ensure that you don't elevate your heart rate too much;
- when running no longer feels comfortable, consider other exercise, such as swimming or aqua-jogging, to keep fit. An exercise bike will help you to keep fit, and may be useful later on if you are at home alone with the baby.

Breastfeeding

If you decide to breastfeed your baby, monitor the baby's weight gain carefully. If the baby does not appear to be putting on weight as quickly as expected, this could be because running is reducing the amount of milk you produce, and you may need to cut back on exercise.

You may usually find it more comfortable for your breasts if you run after rather than before a feed. You can, however, safely breastfeed as soon as you like after running. Immediately after exercise your breast milk may contain lactic acid: this will not harm your baby, but some babies don't like it. You may need to wait for an hour after your run for the lactic acid level to return to normal.

Young runners

Exercise is generally good for young people. Sadly, in most countries of the world, young people are doing less and less. That is one reason why levels of obesity are rising, storing up significant health problems for the future. Young people who exercise are more likely to do well at school and have more self-confidence and a better body image. Girls who run are less likely to suffer from negative images of their bodies; and are less likely to become pregnant as teenagers.

Do you need to start young?

Some sports – such as tennis and swimming – seem to need training from a young age in order to reach world-class status. This is not the case with endurance sports such as running. There is no evidence to suggest that there are physiological benefits to training as children that cannot be obtained by training after the age of 18. Indeed, the opposite is true: children who do well at school often don't go on to perform competitively as adults.

How to avoid doing too much exercise

Young people themselves are usually good judges of how much running they should be doing. Generally, for people under 18, the best advice is to do what you enjoy, and not to train too intensively.

Parents who are themselves keen runners, or who have ambitions for their children, should be careful not to push them too far and too fast. Create the opportunities for your child, but don't put too much pressure on him or her.

As a rule of thumb, children should not train for middle distance races (e.g. 800 m and 1500 m) until they are about 13 or 14; and longer races (e.g. 10 km) should be put on hold until they are 16.

Running injuries occur in young runners as they do for all runners, especially when training levels are increased too fast. Like all runners, young runners shouldn't increase their mileage too rapidly. This can be a particular problem for runners who train mainly at school or at college, if they resume training after a long summer holiday during which they have not run much.

The requirements of young runners

For young people who run occasionally, there is no need to buy specialist running shoes, but if they run more than 10 miles a week, then you should buy appropriate running shoes from a specialist running store.

There are no specific dietary considerations for children who run: they need basically the same diet as any other child. While they should certainly not be eating a diet of high-fat, highly processed food, they should not be prevented from eating foods that are appropriate to growing bodies, including more calories and lots of protein and calcium. Because these often come from foods that are relatively high in fat, an appropriate diet for a young person may well have more calories and more fats than a health-conscious adult would eat.

Children are at greater risk of overheating than adults, because their ratio of body mass to surface area is lower, they sweat less and they produce more heat. So it is important to make sure that young runners drink enough to keep their body temperatures low.

Ten guidelines for parents of children in sports

1 Make sure your children know that – win or lose – you love them and are not disappointed with their performance.
2 Be realistic about your child's physical ability.
3 Help your child set realistic goals.
4 Emphasise improved performance, not winning. Positively reinforce improved skills.
5 Don't relive your own athletic past through your child.
6 Provide a safe environment for training and competition.
7 Control your own emotions at games and events. Don't yell at other players, coaches, or officials.
8 Be a cheerleader for your child and the other children on the team.
9 Respect your child's coaches. Communicate openly with them. If you disagree with their approach, discuss it with them.
10 Be a positive role model. Enjoy sports yourself. Set your own goals. Live a healthy lifestyle.

The Physician and Sportsmedicine *(1988)*

Veteran runners

Running is an excellent sport for people as they get older. It provides significant benefits that can offset the effects of ageing. More than half the runners in the New York City Marathon are over 40.

From your thirties onwards, a number of physical changes take place in the average person's body. Your ability to consume oxygen decreases, muscle mass reduces, muscle elasticity reduces, lung elasticity declines, bone density reduces, the metabolism slows, body fat increases and the immune system becomes weaker.

These changes will have an adverse impact on running performance. The fall in aerobic capacity, reduced stride length, reduced leg strength, and reduced ability to store energy all contribute to a deterioration in performance. In general, it is thought that running speeds deteriorate by about 1 per cent a year from a peak at some point in the thirties; and we appear to lose aerobic capacity at about 9–10 per cent a decade.

However, older runners can continue to perform extraordinary athletic feats. Canadian athlete Ed Whitlock ran a marathon in 2:59:09 in September 2003, at the age of 72. Carlos Lopes set the world marathon record at the age of 38. At the age of 52, Hal Higdon, marathon runner and writer, ran a 10 km in 31:08 and a marathon in 2:29:27.

The benefits of running for older people

The health benefits of running are broadly the same for older people as for everybody else. They include reductions in the risks of heart disease, diabetes, high blood pressure and cancer; reduced depression and anxiety; weight control; improved bones, muscles and joints; improved mobility and co-ordination, and a psychological sense of well-being. What is especially significant for older people is that the risk of developing these conditions grows as you get older, so the benefits of running are increased. It is especially beneficial for older people that running can improve muscle strength, co-ordination and bone density, all reducing the risk of falling and fracturing bones, and so increasing the prospects for living independently.

> 'Age brings problems; it also brings solutions. For every disadvantage there is an advantage. For every measurable loss there is an immeasurable gain.'
>
> *George Sheehan,* Personal Best, *1989*

How to start running as an older person

You are never too old to start running. Running helps to slow down the effects of ageing, improves the health, fitness and mobility of older people, and improves psychological health.

Anyone over the age of 50 should get a check-up by a doctor before they begin any programme of physical exercise (see Chapter 2 for other indications of when it is necessary to get an all-clear from a doctor). In older people, the doctor will be particularly checking for heart disease, diabetes and high blood pressure, to ensure that they can run safely.

Apart from getting a check-up from a doctor, the advice for a new older runner is basically the same as for everyone else, and set out in detail in Chapter 2. The main priorities are to build up slowly, and set yourself demanding but achievable goals.

Tips for older runners

- cut back the mileage, but increase your training quality (there is nothing to stop you from continuing to do fast speed work on the track – this is how Hal Higdon has continued his remarkable performances);
- take more rest days between sessions, and avoid overtraining;
- increase the variety of your aerobic training, for example by aqua-running, cycling, swimming, and skiing;
- warm up carefully before running, and stretch afterwards, to protect muscles, which are less elastic and more prone to injury than they were when you were younger;
- increase your weight training, to compensate for the decline in muscle mass that you would otherwise experience.

Conclusion

My running club has members aged from 17 to over 80 years old. Remarkably, because we share a common interest, there are strong friendships across the years. We have formed deep and lasting relationships that enrich all our lives. Running transcends all ages. For young people, it is a gateway to sports of all kinds. It is an affordable, accessible and safe way to embark on a life of healthy exercise.

As we get older, running helps to reduce the impact of age on our fitness, strength, mobility and independence. It can thereby give us many extra years of good quality of life.

5 Training know-how

Knowing what you are training for

This chapter is about planning your running so that you achieve your goals. You might be running mainly to lose weight, or to reduce stress. You might be running for the health benefits of lower risk of heart disease. Perhaps you have made a bet with yourself or a friend that you can run a 5 km race to raise money for charity. Or perhaps you have rashly promised that you are going to run a marathon.

In Chapter 2 we discussed the importance of setting meaningful goals as a way to keep motivated. Having clear goals is also the cornerstone of a well-designed training programme. A good training programme will help you to improve as a runner, whatever your goals. But as your goals become more specific, so you need to adapt your running to help you meet them. For example, a person training for a marathon would do longer runs than someone wanting to run a 5 km race. If your aim is to lose weight, then you will probably do less speed work than someone who wants to compete in races.

A training programme is going to be effective and sustained only if it is designed around your ability, goals, and other commitments. If you had your own coach, you could work with them to design a programme tailored for you. This chapter will help you to be your own coach, and enable you to design a training programme that suits you. In particular, it introduces the building blocks, which you can put together to meet your own goals, given the time you want to spend running.

How training works

Training makes you a better runner by causing controlled physical stress, which in turn leads your body to adapt.

Your training can improve:

- your cardiovascular system, which provides oxygen to the muscles: this includes strengthening the heart to enable it to pump more blood; improving your lung capacity to enable to you get oxygen into your blood; and improving the amount of oxygen that your blood can carry;
- your running muscles: improvements include increasing the ability of the muscles to turn fuel into movement; increasing the blood supply within the muscle, which brings fuel and oxygen in and takes waste products away; improving the ability of the muscles to store fuel; and increasing the strength, stamina and flexibility of the muscles;
- your metabolic system, which converts carbohydrate, fat and protein into energy: this can be adapted to be able to produce energy more quickly, and to be more efficient at converting fat into energy, providing you with more energy for endurance;
- your joints, ligaments and bones, which adapt to running, increasing their strength and elasticity and your resilience and resistance to injury;
- your running technique, which determines your efficiency in translating muscular output into movement.

Training in different ways stresses your body in different ways, and so emphasises different kinds of adaptation. In other words, you should not think that running as hard as you can every time you put on your running shoes will give you the best improvements in your physical well-being.

Think of a good training programme like a balanced diet. You would not say that protein is 'better for you' than carbohydrate or fat. You need all three. Although you can survive for a while on a diet of one alone, you will not be fully healthy unless your diet includes a mixture of what you need. So it is with training: you need to include a variety of different training types, sometimes in quite small quantities, in order to be fully balanced in the way your body adapts and improves.

'When I was younger, running increased mileage led to improved performance. Frustratingly, after I turned 40 I found that running additional miles did not lead to faster times. And anyway, my other commitments did not permit me to run ever-increasing mileage. I started training on the five-tier pace system after the 2000 Boston Marathon. In the following 12 months, I ran fewer miles per week and set new personal best times for the 5 k, half marathon and the marathon.'

Phil McCubbins,
Hawaii Ironman Finisher, 1999

A training programme for beginners

Before you start

The training programme shown on page 53 is designed for a complete beginner to get from couch potato to running 10–20 miles a week, over a period of six months.

Before you start this training programme, you should have:

- checked whether you need advice from a doctor (see page 11);
- bought yourself proper running shoes and, if you are a woman, a sports bra (see Chapter 3).

In addition, you should remember that:

- it is a good idea to find a buddy who wants to do this with you, so that you can encourage each other; alternatively, start going along to a local running club;
- set yourself a goal which you can work towards;
- the first few weeks of this programme may well seem rather boring and easy, but you should resist the temptation to go any further or faster so that you avoid injury. This programme lays a solid foundation for safe, healthy running in the future;
- if you find that you are not enjoying it for the first few weeks, stick with it. It often takes three to four weeks to really get into running (or to get back into it). For most people, there will suddenly come a time when you realise that it has become easy, and that you really enjoy it.

> '**My advice to new runners? Get a running buddy.**'
>
> *Al Chou,*
> *cyclist and sub-3-hour marathon runner*

About the programme

The numbers shown in the table are minutes a day – not miles! These are intended to give you an idea of how long you should be exercising. It does not matter how fast you go at this stage.

The training programme begins with just walking for the first three weeks. Don't take this too easily: it should be brisk walking, so that you are breathing heavily and perhaps sweating a little. The purpose of the three weeks of walking is to stimulate your bones, muscles and joints to adapt to the exercise, so that they are prepared for when you start running.

Over the next three weeks, we add in an extra five-minute run for each week, for the last five minutes of the walk. Then over the next

6-month training programme for a complete beginner

Week	Mon	Tue	Wed	Thur	Fri	Sat	Sun
1	Walk for 20 minutes every other day						
2	Walk for 20 minutes every other day						
3	W20	W20		W20		W20	
4		W20, R5		W20		W20	
5		W20, R5		W20		W15, R5	
6	W10	W20, R5		W15, R5		W15, R5	
7	W5, R5	W15, R5		W15, R5		W15, R5	
8	W5, R5	W20, R5		W15, R5		W20, R5	
9	W5, R5	W10, R10		W10, R10		W15, R10	
10	W5, R10	W20, R10		W20, R10		W20, R10	
11	W10, R10	W15, R15		W15, R10		W15, R10	
12	W10, R10	W15, R15		W15, R15		W15, R10	
13	W15, R10	W10, R20		W15, R15		W15, R10	
14	W10, R15	W10, R20		W10, R20	W10, R10	W10, R20	
15	W5, R15	W5, R25		W5, R25		W10, R10	
16	W5, R20	R30		W5, R20	R30	W5, R15	
17	R25	R30		R20	R30	R20	
18	R30	R30		R20	R30	R25	
19	R30	R30		R25	R30	R25	
20	R20	R30		R20		R20	
21	R30	R30		R20		R20	
22	R30	R35		R30	R30	R25	
23	R30	R40		R30	R30	R30	
24	R20	R45		R20	R30	R30	

Legend: W10 = walk for 10 minutes; R5 = run for 5 minutes

two months, the amount of running gradually increases, and the walking reduces, so that by week 16 you can do two thirty-minute runs.

It is a common mistake to try to run too fast. Remember the talk test: you should be able to maintain a conversation easily, in complete sentences, on all these runs. If you are too out of breath to speak easily, you are running too fast.

Once you have completed the beginners' training programme, you can look at ways to progress your training.

The building blocks of training

Hill running and leg strength

The speed you run depends on two things: the length of your stride, and your leg turnover (i.e. the number of strides you take per minute). This is blindingly obvious if you think about it, but it has an important implication: if you increase your stride length, you will run faster. To do this you need to improve your flexibility, but also your leg strength so that you push off with greater power for each step.

For longer distance running, leg strength is also a key factor in developing your stamina. Hill workouts strengthen your hamstrings, calves and buttocks, but especially the thigh muscles, which don't get as much of a workout from running on the flat. Marathon runners, in particular, need strong quads to sustain their effort over the full distance. Good leg strength is also a good way to avoid injury. Before you start intense speed training, you should have a base of leg strength which gives you the explosive power you need for speed.

So hill training is valuable for runners of any distance, and especially for longer distance runners. You should plan to

'Having had a tough day at work, I came to training this evening feeling exhausted and run down. By the end of my workout, I felt as if I could take on the world.'

David Ferrier,
runner and theatre manager

increase your hill sessions at the beginning of the training cycle, before you start the serious speed work.

A typical hill session involves finding a hill that is anywhere between 200 metres and 1 km long, with a gradient of between 5 and 15 per cent. Warm up for ten minutes (you may be able to do this by jogging from home to the hill). Then run up the hill hard, keeping your head up and shoulders back. Emphasise your style: push off your feet, lift your knees, and pump your arms hard. As the gradient of the hill changes, try to hold your effort (not your speed) constant. Pump your arms hardest where it is steepest. At the top of the hill, keep running; and jog back down to the bottom and repeat.

If you are new to hill sessions, begin with about a mile of uphill running (plus a mile of jogging down again) and gradually build up to three or four miles. The number of repeats will depend on the length of the hill.

An alternative way to build hills into your schedule is to plan one of your longer routes to include a hilly section (if necessary, repeating a loop of the route with a good hill in it). Again, your aim should be to maintain your effort levels as the gradient increases. Try to ensure that you run a total of at least two to three miles uphill with a gradient of at least 7 per cent.

If you are really stuck for hills where you live, you can sometimes improvise, using a treadmill in your gym (which can be set to a gradient) or stairs at home or in the office.

Threshold runs

Threshold runs – sometimes known as tempo runs – involve running at about your anaerobic threshold (sometimes called your lactate threshold). This is the maximum effort at which your body can work for long periods. It is thought that by training at this level, you can gradually increase the body's capacity to produce energy and its ability to cope with the build-up of lactic acid (which is a by-product of intense exercise).

A threshold run generally consists of a 10-minute warm up, followed by 20–30 minutes of running at just below your anaerobic

> '**What doesn't destroy me makes me stronger.**'
>
> *Friedrich Nietzsche*, Twilight of the Idols
> [Not, apparently, written about threshold runs.]

threshold, followed by 5 minutes of warm-down.

The tricky part is getting the pace right. One way to gauge your threshold run is to find the pace at which you can just hold a conversation. You should be able to talk, but perhaps not in complete sentences. If you are too out of breath to speak at all, you are running too fast, but if you can speak normally, you are running too slowly. You are aiming to run 'comfortably hard'.

If you are an experienced runner, your threshold pace should be somewhere between your 10-mile race pace and your half-marathon race pace, or about 10–30 seconds a mile slower than your 10 km race pace. You can use the calculator at www.runningforfitness.org to calculate the correct pace.

Alternatively, you can use a heart rate monitor to ensure that you do your threshold run just below your aerobic threshold. Your aerobic threshold is generally about 78–85 per cent of your maximum heart rate.

The key to threshold runs is to resist the temptation to go too fast. This is deliberately not a maximum effort workout. As you become fitter, these runs should become easier, until you review your threshold pace and adjust. You should not go as fast as you can from one week to the next: as you feel stronger, you should try to achieve the same pace and distance with less effort.

Fartlek

Fartlek literally means 'speed play' in Swedish (the idea was invented by Swedish coach Gusta Holmer). It means the introduction of faster bursts into a slower run. The purpose of fartlek is to ensure that the whole muscle is getting a good workout; and to build speed and strength.

Fartlek runs can be done as an unstructured session (i.e. running faster as you feel inclined); or in a more structured way (e.g. 10 surges of 400 m). The best place to do fartleks is generally on a trail run or in a park, though some athletes prefer to do them on a track.

A typical fartlek session might be a 10-minute warm-up jog; then hard strides for 3–4 minutes, with 1-minute recoveries, for 10–15 minutes; then a 10-minute jog to cool down.

Another way to do a fartlek is to use landmarks, such as lamp-posts or trees. For example, you might decide to run hard for the next eight lamp-posts, and then jog for a minute. Some running clubs organise fartleks in which different runners take it in turns to lead the group, increasing the pace to hard strides periodically as they see fit, while the rest of the group keeps up with them.

Long runs

The long slow distance run is the cornerstone of any long-distance runner's training programme. Runners call them the 'LSD' – which stands for long, slow, distance run – but the term has stuck because the LSD is one of the most reliable ways of getting the 'runner's high'.

The long run has many benefits. First, it helps to adapt your joints and muscles for endurance. Second, it improves your cardiovascular system, strengthens the heart and increases the blood supply in the muscles; it therefore enhances the body's capacity to deliver oxygen to your muscles. Third, it enhances your body's ability to burn fat as a source of energy. Fourth, it teaches your body to store more energy as glycogen in your muscles. And finally, long slow runs teach the body to run efficiently, minimising the energy expenditure needed to move you along. Even if you are not training for a marathon, the long slow distance run should be a key element in your overall fitness programme.

The LSD run should be run slowly. As well as reducing tiredness and the risk of injury, there are benefits to running slowly which you do not get from running faster. (You would probably be surprised how slowly the best athletes run for their long run.) If you use a heart rate monitor, try to keep your heart rate within 70–80 per cent of your maximal heart rate. It is hard to go too slowly for your LSD; but all too easy to go too fast.

The distance of the long slow distance run depends on the length of the race for which you are training. For a 5 km race, the LSD need not be more than 5–10 miles; but for marathon runners it needs to be more like 20 miles (or longer for advanced runners). Another way of looking at it is that the long run should be between one-quarter and one-third (certainly less than half) of your weekly mileage. So if you are running 20 miles a week, your long run should be around five to seven miles. Unless you are an experienced runner, your long run should not exceed 21 miles.

Track training

Go down to your local running track on a summer evening and inhale the atmosphere. At busy tracks, there will be a hive of activity – with runners, throwers and jumpers, and often people playing team sports on the adjacent pitches. There may also be one or two coaches, with whistles and stopwatches, working with their athletes.

Speed training on a track is unquestionably the most effective way to improve your running performance. The flat surface and measured distance enable you to see exactly how far, and how fast, you have run. By running faster, you build strength in your muscles, and increase your capacity to produce energy quickly. Your running form will improve, increasing your efficiency, and you will learn to relax while running fast. Running on the track is also a time-efficient way to do a hard workout because you compress your effort into a short space of time.

Why train at the track?

- performance
- variety
- convenience and time
- concentration
- safety
- motivation
- access to coaching
- enjoyment.

There are lots of different sessions you can do on the track. Runners have particular terms to describe different types of track workout. The most common are:

- **sprints:** these flat-out runs mainly improve your running form; strides are slower versions of sprints;
- **repetitions** or **repeats:** that is, running fast for a short period, then taking as much time as you need to recover;
- **interval training** (the most common), which is like repetitions except that the focus of the workout is on limiting the rest period ('interval') between each effort; the key to this type of training is that you do not fully recover between efforts. An interval session is defined by the length of the efforts; the pace at which the efforts are run; then number of efforts; and the time permitted for recovery. So a typical interval session might consist of 5 efforts of 1 mile (each mile is 4 laps of a 400 m track) at the speed you could run for 10 km; with a rest of 45 seconds between each effort. This is an excellent session for improving your 10 km times.

The sessions you should do depend on your current level of fitness, and your goals. If you plan to run half marathons and marathons, you should probably run longer intervals at a slower pace than if you are training for a 5 km.

In general you should aim to run on the track once or perhaps twice a week if you are a long-distance runner; and up to five times a fortnight if you are a middle-distance runner or shorter. But you should be aware that track training is physically hard, and therefore the type of training most likely to lead to injury. So you should build up slowly – you should certainly not go from nothing to three times a week in one step.

Easy runs and recovery runs

The key to training is recovery – your body does not adapt while it is under stress, but afterwards when you are recovering. This recovery and adaptation can be enhanced by gentle exercise, which helps to clear the waste products out of the muscles and increase the blood flow. After a hard session or a long distance run, it is usually better to do a recovery run the following day than to rest completely.

Easy runs are typically about 3–6 miles. (Recovery runs after a hard workout the day before should be at the smaller end of this range, lasting around 20–30 minutes.) The easy run should be shorter and faster than a long slow distance run. For experienced runners, they are run at about your marathon pace, or a bit slower. The pace should feel comfortable and you should be able to talk in full sentences easily.

The main risk with recovery runs is that you will run too hard, and so give your body insufficient opportunity to recover. You may want to leave your watch at home, so that you are not tempted to push yourself too much.

Cross training

Cross training means doing exercise other than running, such as cycling, swimming or working out in the gym. All exercise will increase or maintain your fitness and provide other physical benefits, but because the body's adaptation to exercise is quite specific, running is the most efficient way to exercise to improve your running performance.

Nonetheless, cross training can play an important role in your training programmes. The main advantages of doing other forms of exercise are that they increase your overall levels of fitness without adding to the repetitive stress of running. Some exercise, such as swimming and dancing, can also improve your flexibility, and offset some of the tightness caused by running. Cross training can also help to prevent injuries by reducing the extent of muscle imbalance, and by replacing running with non-weight-bearing activities, eliminating some of the impact on the ground. Cross training is also a good way to keep fit while doing things that can include non-running partners, children or other people in your life. You can, for example, go out for a cycle ride with your family or friends.

There is a rule of thumb that runners may find useful when thinking about cross training. Swimming one mile is roughly 'equivalent' (in terms of energy expenditure and benefits to fitness) to four miles of running; and four miles of running are in turn roughly equivalent to 16 miles of cycling.

One particular form of cross training merits particular mention: working out in the gym. Bruce Fordyce, the legendary winner of the Comrades ultra-marathon in South Africa, attributes his success in part to his regular gym workouts.

Weight training can increase the strength and stability of the upper body, which in turn improves running efficiency. It also builds lean muscle, which increases the metabolic rate, reducing fat, and enhances the body's ability to store glycogen.

However, weight training that increases your muscle size increases your weight, which is a handicap for long-distance runners. If you are a seriously competitive runner for whom additional weight is likely to influence your performance, you should use weights in a way that increases your strength and muscle tone but not muscle bulk (i.e. do lots of repetitions with light weights).

Rest

Probably the most important ingredient in your training armoury is rest. It is when you are resting that the body rebuilds muscles and joints, and adapts to the demands it has to meet.

As you increase your running, you are likely to need more sleep. When you are training hard, reckon on an extra hour a night of sleep, especially if you are currently getting fewer than seven hours a night. This extra sleep is a considerable time commitment on top of the time you spend running, and needs to be taken into account when deciding how much training is feasible for you, given the other things you want to do.

Apart from extra sleep, you need to make sure that you are getting enough rest between hard sessions. Never do hard training sessions (e.g. intervals, hills or threshold runs) on consecutive days – you need a day in between to recover.

You should aim to have an easy week once a month, in which you cut back your training volumes by about a third. You should also aim to have an easy month once a year in which you switch to other exercises such as swimming and cycling, and either don't run at all or run only gently, as you feel inclined, without a watch.

Creating the right programme

Many runners are not particularly interested in improving their running performance. For them, the goals of running are primarily to keep fit, lose weight, and reduce stress.

If you have no racing goals, it is still useful to train at different paces to get the best effect of your running on your fitness, because different levels of effort develop your body in different ways.

A programme for all-round fitness should therefore ideally include long slow distance runs, threshold runs, hill training, and speed training. As well as providing holistic improvements in your physical fitness, this variety will help to maintain your interest in running and reduce the risk of injury.

To maintain a good level of fitness, you should run three to five times a week for at least half an hour. If you are designing a training schedule for overall fitness, the 10 km and half marathon schedules should be your benchmarks. These include plenty of aerobic running, including workouts near the anaerobic threshold. Avoid hard sessions on consecutive days, since this increases the risk of injury.

It can be difficult to sustain a training programme of this kind, at least at first, if you don't have a specific goal in mind. One way to do this is to enter a race, perhaps raising money for charity. If you don't want to take part in a race then you might want to set yourself a different, measurable goal. For example, you might want to measure your progress by the fall in your resting heart rate, or your weight.

How many miles should I run?

There is probably no greater topic of controversy among runners than the ideal mileage. As far as we know, basic fitness does not improve if you run more than 50 miles a week. So if you are interested only in increasing your fitness, this is probably the maximum mileage you need to run.

Most runners don't run anything like this sort of distance each week. Clearly, a number of factors affect the optimum mileage:

- lifestyle constraints, such as family and work commitments, and other leisure activities;
- the distances, if any, at which we want to compete (marathon runners need a higher weekly mileage than 5 km runners);
- our capacity to train before we get injured or ill; this is greatly affected by how we train, but there are also some inherited differences.

If your goal is simply to keep fit, then you should be aiming for about 30 miles a week. If you are taking part in a race, overleaf there is a rough guide of recommended mileages for runners of different experience at different race distances. You don't need to run these distances all year round: these are weekly averages in the peak weeks before your race. You should take regular breaks during the year – reducing your mileage, and then build up again.

You should not increase your weekly mileage too rapidly if you want to avoid injury or illness. A very important guideline is that you should not increase your weekly mileage by more than 10 per cent a week. Experience shows that excessively rapid build-up in training mileage is one of the most common causes of injury. Many new runners think that they can be the exception to the rule, because they feel they can go further than this. Sadly, this enthusiasm often ends in tears.

How many times a week to run

If running is your main exercise, you should aim to run three or four times a week, in order to reap the full health benefits. But runners who set themselves more demanding performance goals will need to run five or six days a week, giving themselves one or two rest days.

Elite runners will often run twice a day on at least some days of the week. For example, they may do a track session in the morning, and

Recommended maximum peak weekly distances (miles)

Race distance	Beginner	Intermediate	Advanced
5 km	10–20	15–25	30–40
10 km	15–25	20–30	30–50
Half marathon	20–30	25–35	35–50
Marathon	30–40	40–50	40–60

a recovery run in the evening. These runners may therefore run 10–12 times a week. Even elite runners generally take one day a week off completely, but some rest only one day a fortnight.

Easy weeks

Most runners benefit from cutting back for an easy week, one week in four. In these weeks, the runner should reduce the mileage to about two thirds to three quarters of their normal weekly mileage, while maintaining the speed and quality of the sessions. These easy weeks give your body a chance to recover. If you try to train continuously for more than 12 weeks without some respite, the chances are that you will get ill or injured. It is much better to plan to take an easy week than have one forced upon you.

Putting together training programmes

Earlier in this chapter we set out a training programme for a complete beginner to enable them to get started safely and minimising the risk of injury. Now that you have built up your fitness and stamina, you can progress your running training. A good way to stay motivated is to enter for a race – here are some training programmes to help you do this.

The programmes illustrate how you can put together the various different types of training to get the most benefit for your training. You may well want to put together your own training programme, using these as examples. If you do so, remember the following guidelines:

Things to remember when you design your training programme

- if you are new to running, start with the beginner's programme on page 53;
- limit the increase in mileage to no more than ten per cent of your weekly mileage;
- follow a hard session one day with an easy day the next;
- mix together different types of workout during the week to get the most benefit from your programme;
- build in time to rest: that is the most important workout of the week;
- build a good base of distance and strength before you start speed-work;
- include an easier week every fourth week.

Training schedule for 5 km: beginner

Weeks	Phase	Miles	Mon	Tue	Wed	Thu	Fri	Sat	Sun
Base	Base	13		3 easy	3 thresh			3 easy	4 slow
12	Base	15		4 easy	4 thresh			3 easy	4 slow
11	Strength	16		3 hills	3 easy	3 thresh		3 easy	4 slow
10	Strength	18		3 hills	4 easy	3 fartlek		4 easy	4 slow
9	Strength	19		4 hills	4 easy	3 thresh		2 easy	6 race
8	Strength E	15		3 hills	3 easy	3 fartlek		3 easy	3 slow
7	Speed	18		3 thresh	4 easy	3 interval		3 easy	5 slow
6	Speed	20		4 fartlek	4 easy	4 interval		4 easy	4 slow
5	Speed	20		3 thresh	4 easy	4 interval		4 easy	5 slow
4	Speed E	14		3 fartlek	4 easy	2 interval		2 easy	3 slow
3	Peak	17		3 fartlek	4 easy	4 interval		2 easy	4 slow
2	Peak	11		3 fartlek	3 easy	1 interval			4 slow
1	Race	11		3 strides	3 easy	2 easy			3 race

Sample interval sessions:

Wk 7: 3 sets of 4 x 400 m at 800 m pace; 150 sec recovery between efforts; 1 lap jog between sets

Wk 6: 2 sets of 3 x 1000 m at 3 km pace; 120 sec recovery; 1 lap jog between sets

Wk 5: 400 m, 600 m, 800 m, 1200 m, 1600 m, 1200 m, 800 m, 600 m, 400 m (+5 sec/lap as +distance); 60 sec recovery

Wk 4: 6 x 600 m at 1500 m pace; 120 sec recovery

Wk 3: 4 x 1600 m at 5 km pace; 90 sec recovery

Wk 2: 10 x 200 m at 400 m pace; 180 sec recovery

Training schedule for 5 km: intermediate

Weeks	Phase	Miles	Mon	Tue	Wed	Thu	Fri	Sat	Sun
Base	Base	16		4 easy	3 thresh			4 easy	5 slow
12	Base E	14		4 easy	3 thresh			3 easy	4 slow
11	Strength	18		3 hills	4 easy	3 thresh		3 easy	5 slow
10	Strength	20		3 hills	4 easy	3 fartlek		4 easy	6 slow
9	Strength	22		4 hills	5 easy	3 thresh		4 easy	6 race
8	Strength E	16		2 hills	3 easy	3 fartlek		3 easy	5 slow
7	Speed	23		4 thresh	4 easy	3 interval		4 easy	8 slow
6	Speed	25		5 fartlek	4 easy	4 interval		5 easy	7 slow
5	Speed	25		4 thresh	4 easy	4 interval		5 easy	8 slow
4	Speed E	16		3 fartlek	4 easy	2 interval		2 easy	5 slow
3	Peak	23		3 fartlek	4 easy	4 interval		4 easy	8 slow
2	Peak	17		3 fartlek	4 easy	1 interval		4 easy	5 slow
1	Race	14		3 strides	4 easy	4 easy			3 race

Sample interval sessions:

Wk 7: 3 sets of 4 x 400 m at 800 m pace; 150 sec recovery between efforts; 1 lap jog between sets

Wk 6: 2 sets of 3 x 1000 m at 3 km pace; 120 sec recovery; 1 lap jog between sets

Wk 5: 400 m, 600 m, 800 m, 1200 m, 1600 m, 1200 m, 800 m, 600 m, 400 m (+5 sec/lap as +distance); 60 sec recovery

Wk 4: 6 x 600 m at 1500 m pace; 120 sec recovery

Wk 3: 4 x 1600 m at 5 km pace; 90 sec recovery

Wk 2: 10 x 200 m at 400 m pace; 180 sec recovery

Training schedule for 10 km: beginner

Weeks	Phase	Miles	Mon	Tue	Wed	Thu	Fri	Sat	Sun
Base	Base	16		4 easy	3 thresh			3 easy	6 slow
12	Base E	12		3 easy	3 fartlek			3 easy	3 slow
11	Strength	17		2 hills	3 easy	3 thresh		3 easy	6 slow
10	Strength	18		3 hills	4 easy	3 fartlek		3 easy	5 slow
9	Strength	20		3 hills	4 easy	4 thresh		3 easy	6 race
8	Strength E	14		2 hills	3 easy	4 fartlek			5 slow
7	Speed	21		3 thresh	4 easy	3 interval		3 easy	8 slow
6	Speed	20		4 fartlek	4 easy	4 interval		3 easy	5 slow
5	Speed	21		3 thresh	4 easy	3 interval		4 easy	7 slow
4	Speed E	16		3 fartlek	4 easy	2 interval		3 easy	4 slow
3	Peak	21		3 fartlek	4 easy	4 interval		3 easy	7 slow
2	Peak	16		3 fartlek	4 easy	1 interval		3 easy	5 slow
1	Race	14		3 strides	3 easy	2 easy			6 race

Sample interval sessions:

Wk 7: 3 sets of 4 x 400 m at 800 m pace; 150 sec recovery between efforts; 1 lap jog between sets

Wk 6: 2 sets of 3 x 1000 m at 3 km pace; 120 sec recovery; 1 lap jog between sets

Wk 5: 400 m, 600 m, 800 m, 1200 m, 1600 m, 1200 m, 800 m, 600 m, 400 m (+5 sec/lap as +distance); 60 sec recovery

Wk 4: 6 x 600 m at 1500 m pace; 120 sec recovery

Wk 3: 4 x 1600 m at 5 km pace; 90 sec recovery

Wk 2: 10 x 200 m at 400 m pace; 180 sec recovery

Training schedule for 10 km: intermediate

Weeks	Phase	Miles	Mon	Tue	Wed	Thu	Fri	Sat	Sun
Base	Base	21		5 easy	3 thresh			5 easy	8 slow
12	Base E	17		4 easy	3 thresh			4 easy	6 slow
11	Strength	22		3 hills	5 easy	3 thresh		5 easy	6 slow
10	Strength	24		3 hills	5 easy	3 fartlek		5 easy	8 slow
9	Strength	26		4 hills	5 easy	4 thresh			13 race
8	Strength E	18		2 hills	3 easy	3 fartlek		3 easy	7 slow
7	Speed	26		4 thresh	4 easy	3 interval		5 easy	10 slow
6	Speed	28		5 fartlek	5 easy	4 interval		6 easy	8 slow
5	Speed	29		4 thresh	5 easy	4 interval		6 easy	10 slow
4	Speed E	22		4 fartlek	4 easy	2 interval		4 easy	8 slow
3	Peak	30		4 fartlek	6 easy	4 interval		6 easy	10 slow
2	Peak	19		4 fartlek	4 easy	1 interval		4 easy	6 slow
1	Race	16		3 strides	4 easy	3 easy			6 race

Sample interval sessions:

Wk 7: 3 sets of 4 x 400 m at 800 m pace; 150 sec recovery between efforts; 1 lap jog between sets

Wk 6: 2 sets of 3 x 1000 m at 3 km pace; 120 sec recovery; 1 lap jog between sets

Wk 5: 400 m, 600 m, 800 m, 1200 m, 1600 m, 1200 m, 800 m, 600 m, 400 m (+5 sec/lap as +distance); 60 sec recovery

Wk 4: 6 x 600 m at 1500 m pace; 120 sec recovery

Wk 3: 4 x 1600 m at 5 km pace; 90 sec recovery

Wk 2: 10 x 200 m at 400 m pace; 180 sec recovery

Training session for half marathon: beginner

Weeks	Phase	Miles	Mon	Tue	Wed	Thu	Fri	Sat	Sun
Base	Base	20		5 easy	3 thresh			4 easy	8 slow
12	Base E	15		4 easy	3 fartlek			3 easy	5 slow
11	Strength	20		2 hills	4 easy	3 thresh		5 easy	6 slow
10	Strength	22		3 hills	4 easy	3 fartlek		4 easy	8 slow
9	Strength	24		3 hills	4 easy	3 thresh		1 stride	13 race
8	Strength E	16		2 hills	2 easy	4 fartlek		2 easy	6 slow
7	Speed	25		3 thresh	4 easy	3 interval		3 easy	12 slow
6	Speed	23		4 fartlek	4 easy	4 interval		3 easy	8 slow
5	Speed	25		3 thresh	4 easy	3 interval		3 easy	12 slow
4	Speed E	18		3 fartlek	4 easy	2 interval		3 easy	6 slow
3	Peak	26		3 fartlek	4 easy	4 interval		3 easy	12 slow
2	Peak	20		4 fartlek	4 easy	1 interval		3 easy	8 slow
1	Race	20		3 strides	2 easy	2 easy			13 race

Sample interval sessions:

Wk 7: 3 sets of 4 x 400 m at 800 m pace; 150 sec recovery between efforts; 1 lap jog between sets

Wk 6: 2 sets of 3 x 1000 m at 3 km pace; 120 sec recovery; 1 lap jog between sets

Wk 5: 400 m, 600 m, 800 m, 1200 m, 1600 m, 1200 m, 800 m, 600 m, 400 m (+5 sec/lap as +distance); 60 sec recovery

Wk 4: 6 x 600 m at 1500 m pace; 120 sec recovery

Wk 3: 4 x 1600 m at 5 km pace; 90 sec recovery

Wk 2: 10 x 200 m at 400 m pace; 180 sec recovery

Training programme for half marathon: intermediate

Weeks	Phase	Miles	Mon	Tue	Wed	Thu	Fri	Sat	Sun
Base	Base	24		6 easy	4 thresh			6 easy	8 slow
12	Base E	18		5 easy	3 fartlek			4 easy	6 slow
11	Strength	24		3 hills	5 easy	3 thresh		5 easy	8 slow
10	Strength	26		3 hills	5 easy	3 fartlek		5 easy	10 slow
9	Strength	29		4 hills	5 easy	3 thresh		4 easy	13 race
8	Strength E	21		4 hills	3 easy	3 fartlek		3 easy	8 slow
7	Speed	31		4 thresh	4 easy	3 interval		6 easy	14 slow
6	Speed	30		5 fartlek	5 easy	4 interval		6 easy	10 slow
5	Speed	33		4 thresh	5 easy	4 interval		6 easy	14 slow
4	Speed E	24		4 fartlek	4 easy	2 interval		6 easy	8 slow
3	Peak	32		4 fartlek	4 easy	4 interval		6 easy	14 slow
2	Taper	21		4 fartlek	4 easy	1 interval		6 easy	6 slow
1	Race	24		3 strides	4 easy	4 easy			13 race

Sample interval sessions:

Wk 7: 3 sets of 4 x 400 m at 800 m pace; 150 sec recovery between efforts; 1 lap jog between sets

Wk 6: 2 sets of 3 x 1000 m at 3 km pace; 120 sec recovery; 1 lap jog between sets

Wk 5: 400 m, 600 m, 800 m, 1200 m, 1600 m, 1200 m, 800 m, 600 m, 400 m (+5 sec/lap as +distance); 60 sec recovery

Wk 4: 6 x 600 m at 1500 m pace; 120 sec recovery

Wk 3: 4 x 1600 m at 5 km pace; 90 sec recovery

Wk 2: 10 x 200 m at 400 m pace; 180 sec recovery

6 Nutrition for running

One of the pleasures of being a runner is that you can eat and drink considerably more than if you have a sedentary lifestyle, and still be healthy and avoid putting on weight. Running enables you to escape from the constant hunger, self-denial and self-loathing of dieting, and instead enables you to eat a wide variety of foods more or less as you please.

Nutrition is also the third most important determinant of your running performance, after genetics and training. If you want to be a good runner, you have to eat and drink the right things.

> 'Some people eat to run. Others run to eat.'
>
> *Phil, club runner, 44*

Losing weight

Obesity is a growing problem in Britain, with around half of women and two-thirds of men currently overweight or obese. This can lead to poor health, including heart disease and diabetes, and reduced life expectancy. It also reduces quality of life, both physically and psychologically.

Many runners take up running to lose weight. Runners benefit from a virtuous circle of weight loss, increased self-esteem, improved performance and commitment to a healthier lifestyle.

'For me, running is a means of getting slim in a happy atmosphere.'

James Stratford

Running is an ideal way of losing fat and improving your appearance. It increases your energy consumption, allowing you to continue to eat satisfying amounts of food while reducing your levels of body fat. Conversely, weight loss is an effective way to improve your running. For competitive athletes, reaching the correct body weight is an important component in improving performance.

Why running is a good way to lose weight

Losing weight by exercising increases your energy consumption, so you can continue to eat normally, your body increases its metabolic rate (even when you are not running), you get plenty of key nutrients, and you feel good about yourself. For me it is a no-brainer: if you want to lose weight, take up running.

By contrast, diets are not a good way to lose weight because:

- many people on diets are perpetually hungry, and although they may reduce their food intake for a time, it is unlikely that they will be able to maintain their lower weight;
- the human body reacts to low food intake by reducing its metabolic rate (i.e. your body goes into starvation mode to conserve energy); this defeats the point of the diet since it means that your body slows down your calorie consumption;
- constraining your food intake restricts your intake of key nutrients (e.g. vitamins and minerals), the absence of which can eventually make you ill;
- psychologically, dieting can reinforce a personal sense of self-disgust and dissatisfaction with your own body.

How to reduce your body fat

The principles for losing fat are simple. Your body uses fat to store energy that is surplus to its requirements. So if you take in (i.e. eat) more energy than you use up, your body will store the excess calories as fat. If you use up more energy than you take in, then you will burn stored fat to provide the extra energy.

From the point of view of reducing your body fat, it doesn't matter where the calories come from: a surplus calorie will be stored as body fat, whether it was originally from protein, carbohydrate or fat. So the composition of your food intake is much less important for losing fat than the total amount of calories you consume and the amount of energy you use.

> In other words, to reduce your body fat you must eat fewer calories and/or burn more energy.

Most diets are aimed at getting you to eat fewer calories. This usually means either restricting the total volume of food you eat, or eating foods that contain fewer calories per mouthful, so that you eat as much food but it contains less energy. Some diets are intended to get you to burn more energy by increasing your metabolic rate.

It doesn't matter to your overall weight loss where the calories come from; but if you are going to restrict your calorie intake, it is generally a good idea to cut back on alcohol, harmful fats and refined sugars, so that you continue to include beneficial foods in your diet.

Alcohol is high in calories (about 90 kcal for a glass of wine or 170 kcal for a pint of beer). It is also diuretic (i.e. it makes you urinate), contributing to dehydration. While alcohol is not unhealthy in moderation, it does not do you much good, and cutting back on calories from this source will make you less hungry than cutting back on your basic food intake.

The reasons for cutting back on fats are:

- fat has more than twice as many calories per gram than carbohydrates or protein; so if you cut back on calories by reducing fat, you don't have to reduce the amount of food you eat by so much as an equivalent reduction in calories achieved by cutting out protein or carbohydrate;

■ some fats – such as saturated fats and hydrogenated fats – are positively harmful and so you should aim to reduce these in your diet;

■ most of us eat more fat than we should in the first place; so cutting back on fat often brings us back towards a more desirable, balanced diet.

The reasons for cutting back on refined sugars are that they lead to large swings in blood sugar levels. In children, refined sugar is associated with hyperactivity.

This is not primarily a book about dieting. My own view is that the best way to lose weight is to exercise more. But if you decide to cut back on calories, it seems that the most effective ways to do this are ones that don't leave you feeling perpetually hungry. This means that you need to eat foods that have high volume for each calorie. Hence low-fat, low-sugar, high-fibre diets are likely to be the most sustainable ways to reduce calorie intake.

Burning more calories

Burning more calories is generally a more sustainable and positive way to lose body fat than trying to eat fewer calories. The main ways to burn more calories are to exercise, and, to a lesser extent, to change what and when you eat.

Exercising burns more calories in three ways:

■ first, you use energy during the exercise itself: for example, running or walking uses up about 100 calories per mile – and this is not greatly affected by how fast you go (clearly, you will burn more calories per hour if you run faster, but the number of calories per mile will stay pretty much the same); the table opposite shows the calories burned for other common exercises;

■ second, regular exercise increases your metabolic rate even while you are not exercising;

■ third, exercise increases the amount of lean muscle tissue in your body, and this in turn increases your metabolic rate.

Other ways to increase your metabolic rate (and hence energy consumption) are:

- altering when you eat: in general, a large breakfast seems to kick-start your metabolism so that you burn up more calories during the day; in addition, there is evidence that eating little and often (e.g. 4–5 moderate-sized meals and snacks a day, rather than 2–3 larger meals) maintains a higher metabolic rate through the day;
- changing the time you exercise: exercising in the morning before you have breakfast may increase your metabolic rate during the day by more than exercise in the evening.

There may also be an impact on your metabolism from changing what you eat. For example, your body seems to respond to carbohydrates by increasing your metabolism more than when you eat fats at the same time. However, the size of this compositional effect is probably small enough to ignore.

Calories expended in typical exercises

Activity	Kcal/hour
Aerobics (high intensity)	520
Aerobics (low intensity)	400
Cycling (16 km/hour)	385
Cycling (9 km/hour)	250
Running (6 min/mile)	1000
Running (10 min/mile)	600
Squash	615
Swimming (vigorous)	630
Weight training	270–450

Note: This table assumes a person weighing 65 kg. Calorie consumption would be higher for heavier people

Should you run more slowly to lose more fat?

You may have heard the claim that you should run slowly to burn more fat. My local gym has signs encouraging me to exercise in my 'fat-burning zone'.

This is nonsense. It is true that the proportion of energy that comes directly from fat increases at lower rates of exercise intensity. But this does not mean that you are going to wind up with less body fat if you exercise at lower intensities, for two reasons:

- first, it doesn't matter for your overall level of body fat where the fuel comes from while you are exercising, as your body will replenish and rebalance your energy stores when you are recovering after the exercise. A calorie deficit will always end up reducing your body fat, irrespective of the source of the fuel that you burned during exercise;

- second, what matters is the number of calories that you burn, not the proportion. A higher proportion of the calories may come from fat if you run more slowly, but you are also burning fewer calories in total. If you are able to devote limited time to exercise, you will use up more calories by running as far and as fast as you can in those hours, not by going deliberately slowly.

As we saw in Chapter 5, there are good reasons for running slowly some of the time. But it is not true that you will lose more fat this way.

The main nutrients

As your running progresses you will need to think more carefully about what you eat to support the changing needs of your body.

> The main rule for a balanced diet for a typical healthy adult is to eat from a wide range of unprocessed foods. If you do this, you will not go far wrong.

The main nutrients for human beings are carbohydrates, fats, protein and water.

Carbohydrates

Carbohydrates are mainly used for energy. Foods that are high in carbohydrate include potatoes, pasta, rice, bread, fruit, cereals, pulses and anything sugary.

It is fashionable at the moment to eat a diet that is low in carbohydrate, but there is no scientific reason for doing this, and the majority of mainstream scientists believe that carbohydrates make an important contribution to a balanced diet.

However, there is a case for adjusting the type of carbohydrates that most of us in industrialised societies eat.

Carbohydrates vary in how quickly they are absorbed into the bloodstream. The Glycaemic Index (GI) was originally developed to help diabetics to manage their blood sugar, but it is becoming more widely recognised as a tool for healthy eating.

Examples of high, medium and low glycaemic index foods

High GI foods		Moderate GI foods		Low GI foods	
Food	GI	Food	GI	Food	GI
Glucose	100	All Bran™	42	Chick peas	33
Cornflakes	84	Muesli	56	Green lentils	30
Weetabix	69	Buckwheat	54	Red lentils	26
Brown rice	76	Basmati rice	58	Soya beans	18
White rice	87	Spaghetti	41	Kidney beans	27
Bagel	72	Muffin	44	Apples	38
Baguette	95	Carrots	49	Pears	38
Parsnip	97	Peas	48	Plums	39
Baked potato	85	Baked beans	48	Peanuts	14
Raisins	64	Banana	55	Milk	27
Mars bar	68	Orange	44	Yoghurt	33

Generally, you should eat low-GI meals, because these don't lead to such large variations in your blood sugar and insulin levels. Big swings in your blood sugar can lead to higher levels of body fat, reduced immunity from infection, mood swings and stress, and impaired storage of energy by muscles. However, high GI foods are very useful when you need energy quickly, such as immediately before, during and after exercise.

Unfortunately, the increasingly common diet of processed and packaged foods, and foods that are laced with sugar to make them seem tastier (and which makes them more addictive), means that it is more and more difficult to eat low-glycaemic food. Avoiding these very high-glycaemic foods may be one reason why people who turn to low-carb diets sometimes feel healthier at first and may experience some weight loss.

Fats

Fats are found in oily food, especially animal products, and food cooked in oils. Fats vary in their chemical structure, which in turn makes a difference to how they are handled by the human body and their impact on our health. Some fats are harmful, and some are essential for health. The table opposite summarises the main categories.

Most people in industrialised societies eat more fat than they should; and too much of it is harmful saturated fats. You should be getting around 15–25 per cent of your daily calories from fat, instead of an average of over 40 per cent in Britain. But you should not try to cut fats out of your diet altogether. Try to get most of your fats from mono-unsaturated fats, such as olive oil, nuts and avocados; and ensure that you have sufficient essential fatty acids, which you get from oily fish and seeds.

Protein

Proteins are the building blocks of the human body. About 20 per cent of your body weight is protein. It is mainly needed for growth and repair of body tissues, though it can also be used as fuel for energy. It plays an important role in the health of your blood system.

Types of fat and their health implications

Type of fat	Health implications	Sources
Saturated	Heart disease, increase in cholesterol	Butter, lard, cheese, animal fats. Biscuits, cakes, pastry. Palm oil and coconut oil
Mono-unsaturated	Good for you. Can reduce harmful cholesterol	Olive, rapeseed, groundnut, hazelnut, almond oils. Avocados, olives, nuts, seeds
Poly-unsaturated	Can reduce both good and harmful cholesterol	Most vegetable oils and oily fish
The following fatty acids are specific types of polyunsaturated fat:		
Omega 3 essential fatty acids	Health of blood and blood vessels. Reduced heart disease, lower blood pressure	Oily fish (e.g. mackeral, fresh tuna, salmon, sardines). Linseed (flax), pumpkin seeds, walnuts, rapeseed oil, soya beans
Omega 6 essential fatty acids	Health of cell membranes. But can reduce good cholesterol; high intake may be cancer risk	Vegetable oils, poly-unsaturated margarine

The protein you eat is broken down into amino acids, and then recombined to make suitable human proteins. There are 20 amino acids, of which 12 can be manufactured in the body; but eight of them, called 'essential amino acids', cannot, and they must be obtained from what you eat.

Some foods contain all eight essential amino acids – these include dairy products, eggs, meat and fish. Other foods such as cereals, pulses and nuts have some, but not all, of the essential amino acids and must be eaten in the right combinations to ensure the body has all the components it needs. Vegetarians, and anyone else who does not eat much meat, should ensure that they combine foods from two or more of the following four categories:

- pulses (beans, lentils, peas);
- grains (bread, pasta, rice, cereals, corn, rye);
- nuts and seeds (peanuts, sunflower seeds, pumpkin seeds);
- quorn, tofu and soya products (soya milk, tofu, tempeh, etc).

For example, baked beans on toast is an excellent combination for a vegetarian that provides all the essential amino acids.

If you exercise regularly, and especially if you do strength training, you need to eat more protein than if you are sedentary, to enable you to rebuild and repair muscles.

The current recommended daily intake of protein for a sedentary person is 0.75 g of protein a day for every kilogram of body weight; whereas people who exercise need 1.25–1.75 g of protein a day for every kilogram of body weight.

You can safely eat more protein than this calculation implies, but once your body has used the protein it needs, the extra protein will be burned as energy. (Contrary to what some people believe, your body will not respond by building bigger muscles.)

Eating a balanced diet

Your energy intake should come from a mixture of carbohydrates, fats and protein, made up roughly as follows:

- 15–25 per cent of calories from fat;
- 60–70 per cent of calories from carbohydrates;
- 15–25 per cent of calories from protein.

From these broad proportions, together with an estimate of your overall energy requirements and the amount of protein you need, you can estimate the amount of carbohydrate, fat and protein you should have in your diet. For more information about this, see *The Complete Guide to Sports Nutrition (4th edition)* by Anita Bean (A & C Black, 2003). If you have access to the internet, you can do the calculation for yourself online at www.runningforfitness.org

Vitamins and minerals

Vitamins and minerals are not a source of energy, but they are needed by the body to maintain your health. Inadequate vitamins or minerals can certainly have a harmful impact on your running performance. However, if you eat a balanced diet of largely unprocessed foods, it is likely that you are getting enough of the key vitamins and minerals.

In judging your vitamin and mineral intake you should take the following into account:

- if you are eating packaged or processed foods, they may have fewer vitamins and minerals than fresh food;
- intensive food production (e.g. farming, storage and transportation) means that some foods don't have as many minerals and vitamins as their less intensively produced counterparts;
- if you sweat a lot (e.g. because you are running in a hot climate) you may lose essential minerals in your sweat, which need to be replaced;
- regular exercise increases your vitamin and mineral requirements compared with sedentary people, because they are needed for metabolism, maintenance of tissue and manufacture of red blood cells; the recommended daily allowances (RDAs) that are published by the Government are a guide for the general population, and you may well need to consume more than these guidelines;
- high-intensity training may weaken your immune system, and increased intakes of vitamin C will help to boost your natural defences;

■ it is possible to take too much of some vitamins and minerals (particularly vitamins that are not water soluble, such Vitamins A, B6 and D); large excesses of these can lead to nutritional imbalance and, in extreme cases, serious illness.

On the whole, you should aim to get your vitamin and mineral intake from your diet. However, many active people choose to supplement their diet by taking a multi-vitamin supplement. This provides insurance, in case the vitamins are lacking from the food you eat. But you should not take doses of vitamins or minerals significantly above the recommended daily allowance without first seeking medical advice.

Water

Water is by far the most important nutrient in the runner's diet; and yet most of drink less water than we should. Water is important because it helps to regulate your body temperature (through sweating), and it makes up 82 per cent of blood. Water is also stored with glycogen in your muscles, so if you don't drink enough water your body will not be able to store energy. You can't burn fat if you are too dehydrated. High water intake will also help your body to regulate toxins, and keep your skin healthy.

You need about 1 litre of water for every 1000 kcal you consume during the day (this is your base water intake; you need extra when you are exercising). You also need more in hot or humid weather. This means that if you have a daily calorie intake of 3000 kcal, you need to drink about 3 litres of water each day. That is a lot, and may well be more than you are drinking at the moment. In addition, you lose water through sweating when you exercise. You lose around half a litre for each hour that you exercise – and it can be substantially more than this if it is a hot day.

In deciding how much to drink while exercising, however, you should take account of the fact that water is a by-product of burning fuel to produce energy. This means that your body is producing extra water internally when you are exercising, and you therefore don't need to drink to replace all the water you are losing through sweat.

You should be aware that it is possible to drink too much water, especially during endurance events. There are more documented cases of death from over-hydration than there are from dehydration. Some scientists have concluded that distance runners should drink as they feel (and not force themselves to drink more), which generally means about 500 ml an hour. However, other medical advice recommends drinking rather more than this. For example, the American College of Sports Medicine recommends 600–1200 ml of sports drink an hour. You will have to judge for yourself what works best for you, recognising that there are dangers from over-hydration as well as from dehydration.

On a hot day, you should regulate your temperature by splashing water over yourself as well as by drinking. You may want to pour a cup of water over your head (and especially down the back of your neck), and if you are wearing a cap, make it wet to keep you cool.

When you have finished running, you should aim to replenish the fluid you have lost. Because you don't absorb all the fluid you drink, it is recommended that you drink about half as much again as the volume of fluid you have lost. After a long run, you should try to drink at least 500 ml immediately, and then the rest in slower time.

You should be able to urinate within six hours of completing a long run. If you cannot, it is possible that you have developed kidney failure. If you have not urinated within twelve hours of finishing a long run, contact a doctor. If you are developing kidney failure, the earlier you get medical help the better.

Sports drinks

There is a growing range of drinks that can be used before, during and after exercise (including some other drinks marketed as 'sports drinks' with questionable nutritional credentials).

The main reasons for drinking sports drinks are:

- sports drinks are an effective way to replenish your body's energy levels by providing easily digestible carbohydrates;
- they may replace essential minerals (e.g. sodium, potassium, magnesium, chloride) that you lose when you sweat;

- dilute sugar solutions are absorbed by the body more quickly than plain water, so sports drinks can accelerate fluid replacement;
- drinks containing sodium increase the urge to drink and the palatability of the drink, thereby encouraging you to drink more.

Sports drinks are especially useful for endurance runners during long training runs and races (any run longer than an hour); and for shorter distance runners who want to replenish their energy stores after a tough workout.

Gels

An alternative to using sports drinks to maintain your blood sugar levels is to use gels. These are sachets, sold in specialist running and fitness shops, that contain a sugary syrup designed to be taken during long runs and races. Each sachet contains around 20 g of carbohydrate, so you can usefully take two or three each hour.

The main advantage of gel sachets is that they are easy to carry in a pocket or tucked into the waistband of your shorts, so you can take them on training runs as well as during a race, enabling you to train using the same energy source as that which you will be using on the race day itself. (By contrast, you can't easily do this with a sports drink, since you would have to carry a lot of sports drink on your training runs.)

Most gel sachets should be washed down with water (otherwise they are too concentrated and sickly), so most runners take them as they approach a water aid station. To get the right concentration, you need to wash down a full sachet with about 250 ml of water (more than a full paper cup). If this is too much water to drink in one go while you are running, then take less than a full sachet at each water station. A small amount of gels are isotonic, which means that you don't need to add water.

The different brands of gel are broadly the same (though some also contain caffeine) so try them all and see which you find most palatable. If you decide to use gels during a race, make sure that you use them on your long training runs as well, so that you can find out before the race if they are going to upset your stomach.

Eating after running

After you have finished running you should aim to restock your carbohydrate stores as quickly as possible. This will reduce the risk of illness. In addition, the more quickly you restock your glycogen stores, the more you develop your body's ability to store energy in this form.

In general, the principles for consuming energy after running are:

- aim to eat something quickly – preferably within half an hour, and certainly within two hours; you may well not feel like eating straight away, but you should try to force yourself;
- consume high-glycaemic index carbohydrates, which can be absorbed by the body quickly, such as a bagel with peanut butter, or a sports drink;
- drink plenty of water as well, since this is needed for storage of carbohydrates and to offset dehydration;
- try to accompany the carbohydrates with some protein and fats, since this aids absorption of the carbohydrates. A baked potato with beans or tuna is ideal. If you have had a particularly tough workout, you can use specially formulated 'recovery drinks' which contain a mixture of carbohydrates and protein. You can buy these at your local running shop.

Broadly speaking the best foods to eat immediately after a long run are roughly the same as you should eat before it: plenty of high-glycaemic carbohydrates with a little protein, washed down with lots of water.

Conclusion

Running is one of the healthiest, most sustainable ways to lose weight. Whereas diets are psychologically and often physically damaging, running is a positive and effective way to improve your appearance and health.

A healthy, balanced diet is an essential component of any training programme. If you eat a wide variety of lightly processed or unprocessed foods, you won't go far wrong. You need also to ensure that you drink enough water.

7 Taking it further

Running in races

Running races are not especially competitive. There may be half a dozen runners or so who are in contention to win the race; for the rest of us, races are a way to challenge ourselves, measure our performance, run with other people, and benefit from the race facilities such as traffic-free roads and water tables. The camaraderie among the runners creates a great atmosphere of mutual support. In summary, races are a good day out, and a great way to meet other runners.

Many races give prizes for teams as well as individuals. These are calculated by adding up the position or time of a number of team members, and awarding the prize to the team with the lowest total. Running clubs do not need to choose team members in advance: it is simply the first members of the club to finish who score (e.g. the first four). This means that you don't have to be 'selected' to run for your club. In most races you must be wearing your club's shirt to score for your club.

Competing

George Sheehan, the runner, writer and philosopher, said that the difference between a jogger and a runner is a race entry form.

Not everyone enjoys racing; but every runner should try it a few times. You don't need to be especially fast, or competitive. Very few of the runners in a race has any expectation of finishing first. Races are where we test ourselves, celebrate what we have achieved and face up to our limitations. It's where we engage in a personal struggle with ourselves, supported by the runners around us.

Your first task is to pick a suitable race. Obtain a copy of one of the running magazines (for example, *Runner's World*) that list races; or you can ask members of your local running club. Pick a race in your local area. Generally it is a good idea to start with a shorter distance such as 5 km. Women might consider the Race for Life women's 5 km race series, which raises money for cancer research.

> 'The race is the tournament. It is the trial. The race for me is what the mountain is to the climber, what white water is to the canoeist. The race, where I can be a hero, is a contest where I give my word of honour to go out and do battle with myself'.
>
> *George Sheehan,* Personal Best, *1989*

General racing tips

Running your first race can be pretty scary if you don't know what to expect. Here is the low-down.

- Enter in advance. Most races of half marathon or shorter can be entered on the day, but this can be a hassle. It is better to send off your entry form at least a week before the race, so that you get your race number through the post.
- Plan what to bring. The night before the race, pin your number on your vest, and lay out your clothes on a chair. See the packing list.
- Pin your number on the front of your shirt. Cyclists pin their

number on their back; runners on the front. This enables the organisers to record your finishing time.

> '**I once ran a ten-mile race in a new pair of shoes. After 3 miles I got blisters. I spent the rest of the week hobbling around and couldn't run for a fortnight. So don't wear new shoes in races.**'
>
> *Sally Hodge*

- Arrive early. You don't want to feel rushed. Give yourself at least half an hour – preferably more – to change, go to the toilet, and hand in your bag.

- Start slowly. By far the most common mistake in races is to go shooting off with faster runners. Take it easy at first, and you can speed up towards the end if you still have the energy.

- Don't weave. If you find that the race is congested near the start, don't try to dodge through the runners. Trying to overtake other runners at the start uses up energy, and encourages you to start too fast.

- Enjoy it. Your first race is very special, and you will remember it for years to come.

Packing list

- race clothes
- running shoes with orthotics if you wear them
- running watch
- clean dry clothes, including t-shirt, underwear and socks
- change of shoes
- toilet roll
- Vaseline
- money
- bananas
- safety pins
- race number
- bin liner to wear at start.

Warming up and warming down

The purpose of warming up is to get your body prepared for running. The shorter the race, the more important it is to warm up.

Your metabolism takes some time to adjust to the higher level of energy output you need while you are racing. Your heart rate needs to increase, your blood distribution needs to be redirected to your muscles, and your temperature regulation system needs to adjust. If all this is happening in the early stages of the race, you will be performing below your full potential. If you start a race without warming up, your body will try to produce a lot of energy quickly and will have to use energy systems that produce lactic acid, which will cause you to feel tired quickly during the race.

Ideally, you should start to warm up about 30–40 minutes before the race. Jog a couple of miles, beginning very slowly and gradually increasing the speed to just below your threshold pace. This will get your energy systems working. Then stretch gently for 5–10 minutes, particularly the hamstrings, quads and calf muscles. Finally run up to a mile, at an easy pace but including some strides at your race pace. You should finish your warm-up about five minutes before the race is due to start. If the start is delayed, try to keep yourself moving, by running on the spot if necessary.

The exception to this is a race longer than the half marathon, for which you should do a much lighter warm-up. Because the limiting factor in these races is your energy stores, you don't want to start to deplete your glycogen before the race even starts. You may want to jog for half a mile, working up to your race pace, to get your metabolism going, but you should not do any high-intensity running before the race, as this uses mainly glycogen which you will need later on.

The purpose of 'warming down' is to help your body return to normal after the race, and in particular to keep the blood flowing so that you clear the waste products from your system more quickly. After a short race, you should jog gently for 10–15 minutes at a very easy pace. If you are too tired to do this, you should try to walk briskly instead.

Predicting race times

It is useful to have some idea of how fast you can expect to finish a race, so that you know what pace to start at. If you are an experienced runner, you may be able to predict your race time from previous races, perhaps at different distances (either longer or shorter). There are various equations and tables based on evidence about how much runners slow down as the distance increases to help you do this. These are only guides, although they are sometimes remarkably accurate. You can find these calculations online at www.runningfor fitness.org

Racing 5 km

The 5 km is now a popular distance – partly because of the success in the UK of the Race for Life series of women-only races, which raise money for cancer research. In London, there is a well-attended lunchtime 5 km in Hyde Park on the last Friday of every month.

Races over this distance can be intense; but they don't stress the body as much as longer races, enabling you to continue training or race again the next week if you want to. They are suitable for beginners because they don't require an enormous level of fitness; but they are also an excellent test for more experienced runners.

Although the distance is relatively short, you still need a good base of endurance running and strength for a 5 km training programme, so that you can do the speed training safely and well. Your programme should begin with a month of base aerobic training, then strength training, before you start the speed work.

When you get to the speed work, do plenty of short, fast intervals. While beginners should not do more than one speed session a week, for more experienced runners it is helpful to include a second speed session during the week if possible.

You need to warm up thoroughly for a 5 km race – run at least a mile at moderate pace. Dress in cool clothes, because you will get hot quickly in fast races. It is not necessary to eat or drink in a 5 km race.

Racing 10 km

The 10 km is one of the classic running distances; there are plenty of races at this distance to choose from, and because recovery is quick you can run a 10 km every weekend. The 10 km is an interesting combination of speed and endurance.

Training for a 10 km involves more mileage, and less speed work, than training for a 5 km. To race at this distance you need to be running between 20 and 60 miles a week; and you need a long run of at least 7 miles, and preferably more like 12 miles, at least once a fortnight.

It is a good idea to do some races in the build-up to your 10 km race – perhaps a 5 km for speed, and a longer race (e.g. a half marathon) for endurance. Any race you do during the build-up to a 10 km should not be longer than a half marathon, as this will do you more harm than good.

You should warm up well before a 10 km race. Make sure you drink plenty of water the night before, and up to two hours before the race. Faster runners will not drink at all during a 10 km. Most mid-pack runners should reckon to sip some water once or twice during the race, but you don't need to drink a lot on a race of this duration.

The key to running a good 10 km is running the first mile at the right speed. Too fast and you will throw away your chance of finishing strong in the final miles. Too slow and you will struggle to make up the lost time in the closing stages. My view is that you should run the first mile a few seconds a mile slower than the overall speed you need for your target time.

Many runners sag in the middle stages of the 10 km. At this point you begin to tire; but you are not close enough to the finish to allow yourself to go full out. Concentrate on your form and your breathing, and maintaining a steady pace.

Racing half marathons

This is my favourite distance. The UK's largest mass participation road race is a half marathon (the Great North Run, from Newcastle to South Shields), which reflects the popularity of the distance. It is sufficiently far to be a serious challenge, even to experienced runners. But you can recover from a half marathon in a fortnight, unlike the marathon, from which it can take several months to recover fully.

The half marathon pace is very close to your aerobic threshold, which means that running at this pace enhances your overall aerobic performance, and so improves your fitness and running at all distances. The half marathon is also an essential stepping-stone for anyone interested in running a full marathon. It builds confidence and racing experience, and helps you to judge what you will be able to achieve in a longer race.

If you want to train seriously for a half marathon you will need to do at least 16 weeks of training, beginning with at least a month of aerobic running. Beginners should be running 30 miles a week, and the most serious runners about 60 miles a week. Runners of all standards need to include a long run at least three times a month, of between 10 and 18 miles.

Speed training for a half marathon involves slower, longer repetitions than for the 10 km, with efforts between 800 m and 3 km. It is a good idea to race a 10 km in the build-up to your half marathon, to test your endurance and sharpen your speed.

You should reduce your running considerably in the last two weeks before a half marathon race. This tapering will help you to build muscle glycogen and rehydrate, and ensure that your legs are fresh for the race.

Because this is a long race, you don't need to warm up much before the start. Your task is to preserve your stored energy. You may want to jog for half a mile before the race to loosen up your muscles and get your metabolism going, but you should not do any intense running before the start.

All runners should drink water during a half marathon. The general guidelines on drinking during races apply: drink little and often, right from the gun. Drink as you feel, but don't wait until you feel thirsty to start drinking.

The half marathon is long enough to give you plenty of time to

> '**Don't worry about the miles you have that are behind you: only think about the miles you have still to go. Keep focused on what is ahead. That is the best way to get your pacing right.**'
>
> *Nick Slade, ultra-marathoner*

catch up if you start slowly. The pace of a half marathon will generally seem slow at first, because you are used to running faster for short runs. But if you go off too fast, you will pay the price in the closing stages of the run. You are racing at your aerobic threshold – if you push too fast you will kick into anaerobic metabolism and lactate build-up, and once you have 'blown' you will find it very difficult to regain your equilibrium.

So go out slowly, and ease into the race. Try to get in step with some other runners who are going at about your pace. Let runners go past you for the first few miles: you will probably overtake them in the last few miles. After the second or third mile (not before) you should reach your target pace, which you can hold for most of the race. Try to avoid sagging during miles 6–9. Don't just keep pace with the runners around you, because they might well be slowing down during the second half, just when you should be speeding up.

At the ten-mile mark, you have only the equivalent of a 5 km to complete. Begin to increase your pace, identify runners ahead of you and begin to close them down. Don't accelerate too much – try to remain on the right side of your threshold. In the final mile, push hard, and remember all the speed work you have done on the track.

Injuries

Health risks from running

We don't know as much as we should about the long-term impact of running on your joints. Some studies show that people who have run consistently over many years have a lower risk of joint problems such as arthritis than their sedentary counterparts.[1]

Running does put more stress on your joints than swimming, cycling or skiing, because of the repeated impact of hitting the ground. These risks can be reduced by using good quality and appropriate running shoes (see Chapter 3), running on softer surfaces such as grass or trails when possible, and by starting running slowly.

As for the heart, the evidence is unambiguous: runners are less likely than non-runners to suffer from heart disease. Admittedly, if a runner is going to have a heart attack (e.g. because of an inherited predisposition to heart disease) then it is more likely to happen while they are running than at other times of day, since this is when their heart is under most stress.

Jim Fixx, the father of jogging, famously died of heart disease at the relatively young age of 51. But before he began jogging he had been a heavy smoker, and he had very high blood cholesterol. Jim Fixx survived longer than his father, who died from a heart attack at the age of 43. So our best guess is that regular exercise lengthened Jim Fixx's life

Running is good for you. However, runners often push themselves near to their limits, which means that, although they are in generally better shape than couch potatoes, they get more injuries than they would if they spent their day watching TV. Because runners are stubborn, and sometimes a little obsessed, they often don't do what they should to avoid injuries, and they don't treat them properly when they occur.

Overuse injuries

Runners often suffer from injuries that can be loosely grouped together as 'overuse' injuries – that is, they are not caused by an external force or accident, but appear to be the result of many miles and hours of running. Many of these injuries are caused by (often minor) biomechanical imbalances and defects that, when combined with running, lead to stresses on joints, muscles and other tissues. The cure for these injuries is very rarely found by addressing the symptoms: instead it is necessary to identify the underlying problem.

'Soon after I started running, just as I was really starting to enjoy it, I had to stop for six months because of injury. First I got tendonitis in my groin because I pushed myself too hard every time I went running, instead of interspersing easy runs between hard sessions. Then I got an inflamed Achilles tendon because I increased my mileage too rapidly. Looking back, I wish I had been more patient and built up a firm base of fitness, and invested more in what may seem like side issues, such as flexibility and core stability before trying to build up my mileage. And because I'm relatively new to running, I've realised I should concentrate on shorter distances at first. The main lesson for me is that you have to listen to your body – if it hurts all the time, you are doing something wrong. One week's missed training is better than 6 months moping about not being able to run at all.'

Matt Siddle, 24

The trouble is not that we run too much. On the contrary, because so many of us have sedentary lifestyles, including long hours sitting in chairs, we develop weaknesses and imbalances that then cause problems when we run. The underlying cause of overuse injuries is generally not running (though it is running that triggers the symptoms), but the deterioration in the strength and flexibility in our bodies the rest of the time, as a result of our sedentary lifestyles, that prevents us from running efficiently and without pain.

The good news is that many of these problems are easy to fix, if you get the right advice and tackle the underlying causes rather than the symptoms. The bad news is that all too few doctors know how to do this.

Five steps for avoiding injury

1 **Start running slowly.** People who are new to running and try to do too much too soon will usually become injured, often in their third month of running (see Chapter 2 for more information about starting out).

2 **Get the right running shoes.** By far the biggest cause of overuse injuries is overpronation, which can usually be corrected by choosing appropriate running shoes. Unfortunately, many sports shops don't know how to sell you the right shoes. See Chapter 3 for more information.

3 **Get a check-up** by a sports physiotherapist and podiatrist. This may sound excessive for a hobby runner, but it could well save you from considerable pain, frustration and expensive treatments later. A good sports clinic will make a videotape of you running on a treadmill, and use this to assess your running pattern (sometimes called gait analysis).

4 **Stretch.** Maintaining flexibility will reduce your risk of injury.

5 **Never just 'run through' pain.** As you become a more experienced runner you will learn to distinguish the normal aches and pains that are associated with hard training and effort, and pain that is your body's way of telling you that there is something wrong. When you experience discomfort, don't just keep running and hope that it will go away – the chances are that it will become worse. Nor should you simply stop running – whatever caused the problem will do so again when you return to running. See a specialist who can help to identify the cause, so that you can tackle it (often a straightforward matter of different shoes, simple exercise and stretches, or orthotics in your shoes) before it creates a serious problem.

Avoiding injury

Overuse running injuries are not caused by bad luck; and runners should not be fatalistic about them. Most are caused by an identifiable and avoidable biomechanical problem, often excessive pronation. You cannot completely eliminate the risk of injury – but the box on page 99 provides some key steps you can take to reduce the risks.

Core stability

The biomechanical weaknesses that cause overuse injuries occur primarily because our lifestyles are not consistent with the range of activities for which the human body evolved. For example, because the average city dweller spends large parts of every day sitting down, his or her thigh muscles (*quadriceps*) become elongated and hamstrings too short. Because of our lack of physical activity, muscles are underused and become too weak, or are sometimes not fired (recruited) at all.

You may be thinking to yourself that none of this applies to you, because you are fit, you run and you go regularly to the gym. You are very likely in a better position than the average sedentary person. But we are increasingly coming to understand that the dynamic exercises we do while running or working out address only part of the problem.

Some physiotherapists suggest that we need to pay more attention to our core stability – that is, the ability of key muscles around the abdomen, pelvis and back to hold the torso steady. The muscles that do this are not the large surface muscles that are used in exercises such as sit-ups or leg curls. They are deeper muscles, designed to hold the body steady rather than generate movement. In people who get injured, it appears that these muscles fire late, or not at all, and are too weak to perform their stabilising function. It is clear that having good biomechanics depends on the proper functioning of these key muscles around our lower trunk, and on all our muscles being properly recruited, the right length and sufficiently strong and flexible.

Core stability is a deceptively simple but important idea. It tells us that we should look for the causes of injuries, not in our running, which is consistent with the evolution of the human body over millions of years, but in the weaknesses and imbalances in our bodies caused by the lifestyles we live today for which our bodies are not well adapted.

Treating minor injuries

It is difficult to generalise about what you should do if you get an injury – so much depends on the nature of the injury and the probable cause.

For minor niggles that you can treat yourself, remember the golden rule: RICE – Rest, Ice, Compression and Elevation. For anything that lasts more than a day or two, or that causes severe discomfort, pins and needles, paralysis, sharp localised pain or discolouration, seek medical help as quickly as possible.

Stretching

The scientific community does not fully agree on the benefits of stretching. The current wisdom is that static stretching before you train is unlikely to be beneficial, and may even be harmful; but that stretching after you run may improve muscle recovery and reduce muscle soreness. You should, however, always warm up before running hard.

In addition, as many runners who stretch will attest, maintaining flexibility makes you feel better, improves running performance and reduces the long-term risk of injury. Stretching can also contribute to a programme of developing core stability by correcting imbalances in muscle length that lead to poor biomechanics. So in general, runners should stretch more, though they don't need to combine stretching in the same workout as running.

Most people prefer to stretch warm muscles, and do some light jogging or cycling to warm up before they stretch. However, there is no evidence that warm muscles can be stretched more easily than cold muscles, nor that warming up before stretching reduces the risk of injury.

The days of bouncing up and down to touch your toes are over. Rapid movements trigger a 'stretch reflex' in the muscle being stretched, which causes it to contract. Just as you are trying to lengthen the muscle, it is trying to contract, and you will put undue stress on the muscle. So you are at considerable risk of injury if you try to stretch by bouncing up and down. Instead, you should gradually stretch out the muscle, and hold the stretch while breathing deeply. After 20 seconds or so, the muscle tension falls, and you should be able to stretch the muscle a little more. Remember to breathe deeply, and push the stretch a little further as you breathe out. Hold the stretch for about 60 seconds in total for each muscle.

Don't expect immediate results from stretching. The benefits take time to build up. But once you have increased your flexibility, it can be maintained with much reduced levels of stretching.

8 More information

Now that you have started to run, you may well want to find out a bit more.

Clubs

A running club should be your first port of call. As explained in Chapter 2, running clubs are not just for serious runners. Most running clubs cater for runners of all levels.

In any running club you will find unrivalled experience and expertise, and a willingness to share it. I have learned more about running from my running buddies, and fellow members of the Serpentine Running Club, than from reading mountains of books and scientific journals.

Books

What follows is a very personal list of books that you might like to read if you want to find out more about running.

Owen Barder, *Running for Fitness* (2001)
A more complex version of this book, *Running for Fitness* enables intermediate-level runners to design their own training programme, using techniques from professional athletes. The accompanying

website, www.runningforfitness.org, contains details of the calculations and how to use them.

Anita Bean, *The Complete Guide to Sports Nutrition* (2003)
Anita Bean is a former body-builder, whose book is comprehensive and easy to read. It is packed with examples (including menu plans) to bring the theories to life. Bean is not afraid to roll up her sleeves and she gets stuck into the biochemistry, but everything is presented in an approachable way.

Jack Daniels, *Daniels' Running Formula* (1998)
Jack Daniels' book is a must-have classic that should appear on the bookshelf of every serious runner with a scientific bent. Daniels' approach is to divide training into five quite precise zones, based on the runner's VO2 max. All training should happen in one of those zones (and by implication, any running outside one of these zones is junk miles). Daniels also proposes a complex programme of periodisation of training to obtain the best benefits. The book is based on a great deal of scientific research, and is quite numerical.

Jeff Galloway, *Galloway's Book on Running* (1984)
The top-selling book in the world on running, this is a standard text. In the current version it covers training for the 5 km, 10 km and half marathon (if you want to know about marathons you'll have to buy a separate book, *Marathon: You Can Do It!*). Galloway's approach can occasionally seem a little old-fashioned, but there is a lot of good sense in this book.

Bob Glover and Shelly-lynn Florence Glover, *The Competitive Runner's Handbook* (1983)
A comprehensive book tightly packed with useful information for runners who want to race. The Glovers are leading lights in the New York Road Runner's Club, and Bob Glover has thirty years' experience of coaching. A book to dip into, rather than read in a single sitting.

Hal Higdon, *Marathon: The Ultimate Training Guide* (1999)
Hal Higdon is a runner and writer, contributing a popular column for Runner's World magazine. He also organises training camps in the US for runners who want to run a marathon. His book on the marathon is a classic, which has inspired thousands of people to take to the roads. Simple and well written, in a chatty style, it draws on his deep reservoirs of knowledge and experience. Higdon has written more than thirty other books, including *Smart Running*, which contains lots of useful material, but in a slightly irritating question and answer format.

Frank Horwill, *An Obsession for Running* (1991)
Horwill's slim volume describes his own odyssey, including his fight with stomach cancer, while explaining the theory behind his five-pace training theory. More than anyone else, Horwill was the drive behind the renaissance of English middle distance running in the 1970s and 1980s. Peter Coe (Sebastian Coe's father and coach) credits Horwill with the breakthroughs in training on which Coe's remarkable career was built.

Tim Noakes, *The Lore of Running* (2001)
This is the ultimate runner's reference book. Tim Noakes is a marathon runner, and Professor of Sports Science at the University of Cape Town. Noakes covers each issue comprehensively, setting out the evidence and then proposing his own conclusions (but always distinguishing his own comments from the facts). The latest edition was published in 2001, and has been significantly revised.

Pete Pfitzinger and Scott Douglas, *Road Racing for Serious Runners* (1999)
This is an excellent practical manual for training for races from 5 km to the marathon. The book assumes a reasonably high starting point, both in terms of running ability and knowledge about the subject. The approach owes much to the techniques of Jack Daniels, and the book sets out simple and specific training programmes. It is clearly

and simply written. Unusually (and unexpectedly, given the title) there is advice on training for cross-country.

George Sheehan, *Running to Win* (1992); *Personal Best* (1989); *Running and Being* (1978)
George Sheehan was a medical doctor who took up running in his mid-forties. Five years later he set a world record for the mile for a 50-year-old (4:47). He ran more than 60 marathons, including a personal best of 3:01 at the age of 61. In 1968 he began to write about running for a local newspaper; ten years later his book *Running and Being* became a national bestseller. He established himself as the foremost philosopher of running, with a knack for expressing in words the ideas that many runners have subconsciously about their running. Sheehan's books are an absolute inspiration for every runner. He died in 1993.

Websites

Amateur Athletics Association
http://www.englandathletics.org.uk/

Athletic Association of Wales
http://www.welshathletics.org/

Athletics Weekly
http://www.athletics-online.co.uk/

British Milers Club
http://www.britishmilersclub.com/

British Triathlon Association
http://www.britishtriathlon.org/

British Veterans Athletic Federation
http://www.bvaf.org.uk/

Central Council of Physical Recreation
http://www.ccpr.org.uk/

Directory of UK Podiatrists
http://www.podiatrypages.co.uk/

Hal Higdon's Marathon Training
http://www.halhigdon.com/

Less Bounce Sports Bras
http://www.lessbounce.com/

Northern Ireland Athletic Federation
http://www.niathletics.org/

Peak Performance Online
http://www.pponline.co.uk/

Run the Planet
http://www.runtheplanet.com/

Runner's World
http://www.runnersworld.co.uk/

Runner's World Women's Running
http://www.womens-running.com/

Running for Fitness
http://www.runningforfitness.org/

Scottish Athletics
http://www.saf.org.uk/

Serpentine Running Club
http://www.serpentine.org.uk/

Sports Aid
http://www.sportsaid.org.uk/

Sports Coach
http://www.brianmac.demon.co.uk/

Sports Injury Clinic
http://www.sportsinjuryclinic.net/

Tales of the Penguin (John Bingham)
http://www.waddleon.com/

The London Marathon
http://www.london-marathon.co.uk/

UK Athletics
http://www.ukathletics.net/

UK Athletics Club Directory
http://www.runtrackdir.com/ukclubs

UK Results
http://www.ukresults.net/

UK Running Track Directory
http://www.runtrackdir.com/

UK Sport
http://www.uksport.gov.uk/

World Masters Athletics
http://www.world-masters-athletics.org/

References

Chapter 1: Why run?
[1] Health Development Agency, Health Promotion Effectiveness Reviews, Summary Bulletin 14 (1998)

[2] National Audit Office, Obesity in England, Office of the Comptroller and Auditor General. February 2001

[3] Report of a WHO Consultation on Obesity, 3–5 June 1997, Geneva, WHO/NUT/NCD/98.1

Chapter 7: Taking it further
[1] Tim Noakes, *The Lore of Running* (Oxford University Press, 2001)

Glossary

Adaptation The process by which the human body changes in response to stress. Training is aimed at creating adaptations such as a healthier heart.

Aerobic capacity The ability of a person to take in oxygen and get it to the muscles that need it to make energy. Aerobic capacity is a reasonable measure of overall fitness.

Aerobic threshold The highest intensity of exercise at which the body is mainly getting energy from adding oxygen to carbohydrates. At high intensities, the body cannot get enough oxygen and has to switch to *anaerobic* energy sources, which cannot be sustained for long.

Amenorrhea Erratic or absent periods.

Amino acids The chemical building blocks of protein.

Anaerobic threshold The level of exercise intensity at which lactic acid starts to accumulate in the muscles faster than it can be cleared. Heart rate will be about 20 beats per minute higher than it is at the aerobic threshold.

Balanced diet A diet that contains broadly the right amount of the nutrients that a person needs.

Biomechanics The operation of the skeleton, muscles and tendons to move the human body around.

Calorie A measure of energy, often used to describe the energy content of food. A 'calorie' is the amount of heat required to raise the temperature of one gram of water by one degree Celsius. A kilo-calorie, or 'Calorie' (note the initial capital) is a thousand times bigger, i.e. the amount of heat required to raise one kilogram of water by one degree Celsius.

Cardiovascular fitness The ability of the heart, lungs and blood vessels to deliver oxygenated blood to the rest of the body. Cardiovascular fitness is a major determinant of a person's risk of heart disease and stroke.

Cardiovascular system The heart, lungs and blood vessels.

Cool-down Gentle exercise after a run, aimed at bringing the body's systems gently back to normal.

Core stability The proper functioning of the muscles, mainly around the abdomen and lower back, to stabilise the torso when the limbs move.

Cross training Doing a different exercise from your 'main' exercise to improve fitness, e.g. cycling as a component of your running programme.

Dehydration A condition of inadequate water in the body. Severe dehydration can be fatal.

Easy run A run whose aim is to stimulate the flow of blood and gently elevate the heart rate, and so is best done without a watch. You should be able to talk easily with your running buddy when you do an easy run.

Efficiency The ability to turn energy into motion. Efficient runners cover more ground for the same amount of energy than less efficient runners.

Endorphins A group of hormones produced by the body that affect mood, perception of pain, memory retention and learning. Chemically similar to opium-derived narcotics, endorphins are the brain's own natural painkillers. Endorphins contribute to euphoric feelings such as the 'runner's high' experienced after prolonged exercise.

Endurance The ability to exercise for a long time.

Essential fatty acids Fatty acids that the body is unable to produce on its own, but which are necessary for the proper functioning of cells. They must therefore be obtained from the diet. Rich sources of essential fatty acids include fish, nuts and seeds.

Fartlek Literally 'speed play' in Swedish, fartlek is variable pace running. It usually consists of running at a moderate pace interspersed with short, fast bursts. It increases speed and endurance.

Flexibility The ability of muscle tissue and connecting tissues in the human body to allow a full range of movement. Important for avoiding injuries.

Glycaemic Index (GI) A measure of how quickly the energy in a particular food reaches the bloodstream. A high GI means that the energy is quickly absorbed, while low GI foods release energy slowly over a period of time.

Glycogen A chemical made by the human body to store energy. Consists of a chain of glucose (sugar) molecules.

Heart rate training zones You can measure the intensity of your exercise according to how fast your heart beats. Your training should be made up of mainly low-intensity exercise (which means a low heart rate) with a small amount of high intensity exercise each week. You can devise zones, based on your own maximum and minimum heart rate, to guide you.

Hill training Doing some of your running on hills will increase your leg strength and your fitness.

Interval training A combination of high-energy exercise followed by a period of low-intensity activity. The focus when doing interval training is on setting the right rest period (the 'interval') between efforts. Interval training is especially effective at improving the cardiovascular system.

Lactic acid Lactic acid is produced in the body as a result of high-intensity, anaerobic exercise and creates a sensation of fatigue in the muscle. The build-up of lactic acid is sometimes claimed to be a constraint on the speed and distance of middle-distance (e.g. 800 m and 1500 m) runners.

LSD runs Long slow distance runs are a key element of almost every runner's training. They build endurance and improve overall fitness. As well as being the acronym for 'long slow distance', LSD runs are so-called because some runners achieve a pronounced 'runner's high' from these runs.

Maximal heart rate An individual's highest achievable number of heart beats per minute. This is largely genetically determined (it does not depend on fitness), and falls slightly with age. A maximal heart rate test should only be performed if there are no significant risk factors for a heart condition.

Metabolic rate   The speed at which the body can translate food into energy.

Metabolism   The process of building the body's molecular structures from nutrients (anabolism) and breaking them down for energy (catabolism).

Monounsaturated fats
Monounsaturated fats are made up of fatty acids that contain a double bond in the carbon chain, so that they are not 'saturated' with hydrogen. Monounsaturated fats are typically liquid at room temperature, but solidify when refrigerated.

Muscle imbalances   Muscle imbalances occur if one muscle group is stronger, weaker, more flexible or less flexible than it should be, resulting in an uneven motion of the body. The repetitive action of running, combined with muscle imbalances, can cause overuse injuries.

Muscle tone   The degree of tension in the resting muscle. Muscle tone affects not only our posture, but also our facial expressions, our voice, the control we have over our eyes, and so on.

Overhydration   Overhydration, also called water excess or water intoxication, is a condition in which the body contains too much water and

is sometimes the result of a runner in a long endurance race over-compensating and drinking too much. In extreme circumstances, over-hydration can lead to the life-threatening condition of dilutional hyponatremia (low blood sodium concentration).

Overpronation   The very common tendency for the foot and knee to roll in too much during the landing phase (i.e. when the foot hits the ground) while running. Some pronation is normal and desirable, but uncorrected overpronation can lead to a range of overuse running injuries. Overpronation can be reduced by choosing the right running shoes.

Oversupination   Much less common than overpronation, oversupination is a tendency for the foot to roll out too much during the take-off (i.e. when the foot leaves the ground) phase of running.

Overtraining   Overtraining is a general term for a complex set of symptoms, ranging from fatigue to diarrhoea, and typically including sharply reduced running performance and enjoyment. Overtraining is cause by insufficient rest, or a too-rapid build-up of running mileage.

Overuse injuries   Injuries arising from the repeated action of running (as opposed to an accident).

Pace   The inverse of speed – that is, minutes per mile (as opposed to miles per hour).

Pronation   The rolling action of the foot during the landing phase of each step, to absorb the shock of the impact. (See also *overpronation*).

Recovery runs   Recovery runs should be performed the day after a hard session, as they are designed to help the body clear the waste products caused by heavy exercise and stimulate blood flow to aid the rebuilding of tissues.

Repetitions   Usually done on a track (but can be done in a park), a repetition is a hard effort – such as a sprint – for a short time, followed by a recovery. In repetitions (as opposed to interval training) you can usually take as much time as you like to recover.

Resting heart rate   The heart rate when at rest. Typically lower early in the morning, before you get out of bed. The resting heart rate is elevated by caffeine, excitement and so on. An individual's resting heart rate varies according to fitness (unlike the maximal heart rate), but a person with a low resting heart rate is not necessarily fitter than someone else with a higher resting heart rate.

Running form   A person's style of running, which determines, among other things, their running efficiency and their susceptibility to injury. Running form can be improved by track training.

Saturated fats   Fats that contain no carbon-to-carbon double bonds. They are more stable than unsaturated fats, which is why they are popular in the food industry. They are typically solid at room temperature. They come mainly from animal sources (beef, whole-milk dairy

products, dark-meat poultry) but also from tropical vegetable oils (coconut, palm). Saturated fats are the main dietary contributors to raised blood cholesterol levels and over-consumption of saturated fats is an important risk factor for heart disease and cardiovascular problems.

Speed training   A form of training that emphasises running at high speeds for a short time, usually on a track. An important part of a training programme, but should only form a small proportion of total running mileage.

Tempo runs   The majority of runners use this term to mean the same as a threshold run: that is, a run that includes about 15–20 minutes of running at your aerobic threshold. Tempo runs are a particularly efficient way of improving your cardiovascular system. (Some people use this term to mean something completely different: namely runs at a target race pace.)

Threshold runs   An alternative term for tempo runs.

Tread   The indented part in the sole of a shoe, which is intended to reduce the risk of slipping.

Warm-down   The same as 'cooldown' – gentle exercise after a hard effort to allow the body to adjust gently back to rest.

Weight training   Using weights to develop specific muscle groups. Usually done in a gym, but can be done at home using makeshift alternatives (e.g. bags of sugar).

Index